More Advance Praise for *A Survival Guide to Parenting Teens*

"Joani is down-to-earth, witty, and wise—qualities that you will find in abundance throughout her wonderful book. *A Survival Guide to Parenting Teens* reads like a conversation with a good friend who is right there when your teen is struggling with all the usual and unusual things that parents face on a regular basis."

—Dan Kiley, Director of Community and
Cultural Program, The Fessenden School

"With honesty, authenticity, and authority, Joani portrays the full landscape of teenage emotion, angst, conflicts, and challenges that confronts teens and their parents. Through insight, humor, real-life examples, and action scripts, Joani turns conflict into conversation, reproach into respect, and hassle into harmony. As the parents of three boys, now grown men, we only wish we could have been guided by this superb book."

—Marlene Linkow, Teacher, and Peter Linkow,
President Emeritus, Work-Family Directions, Inc.

"Refreshingly honest and practical, Joani Geltman gets the inherent conflict in families as teenagers assert their independence. She effectively uses humor to defuse the loaded parent/teenage relationship. Great book full of practical strategies."

—Mary E. Dolbear, Middle School Director,
Buckingham Browne & Nichols School

"Every spring we invite Joani back to Brookline to speak to our incoming 9th grade parents, preparing them for their teen's transition to high school. How wonderful that all parents can now have the "Joani advantage" with this new book."

—Mary Minott, LICSW, Social Worker, Brookline High School

"We have had Joani speak at our 9th grade parent assembly for years. She talks with refreshing honesty to parents about the inner life of teens and the all-too-real fears of parents. *A Survival Guide to Parenting Teens* is direct, funny, and insightful. I rely on Joani's words a great deal both at school and at home with my own kids."

—Paul DiDomenico, Assistant Principal,
Algonquin Regional High School

"What a terrific resource for parents of teenagers! Joani Geltman brings her extensive experience right down to practical solutions to everyday problems. Her vast understanding of the angst of adolescents will promote greater understanding and empathy for this challenging stage of life."

—Caroline MacNichol, Director of the
Middle School, Dana Hall School

"For many years, Joani has been our beloved village maven on teenage-hood; now she can be your maven too through this book. Joani's unique blend of direct, no-holds-barred news from the front line, coupled with her thoughtful and wise strategies for successful parent/teen dynamics, makes *A Survival Guide to Parenting Teens* an essential tool in any parent's toolbox."

—Kathleen Maguire, Community Engagement
Manager, In Control Crash Prevention

"Joani speaks the language of today's teens. She is uniquely able to help parents decipher their behaviors that both mystify us and make us crazy. Her entertaining delivery is half the fun. She helps us laugh at our insecurities and reassures us that all will be well at the end."

—Nancy Doyle and Jennifer Sage, President and
Vice President, Thayer Academy Parents Association

"Joani Geltman has a gift for capturing the complexities of raising teenagers in our fast-paced culture and conveying practical and sensible advice. *A Survival Guide to Parenting Teens* has parents at turns laughing hysterically at familiar situations and reading hungrily for the solutions."

—Michael Daly, Director, Resiliency For Life

a survival guide to parenting teens

a survival guide to parenting teens

talking to your kids about sexting, drinking, drugs, and other things that freak you out

Joani Geltman, MSW

AMACOM AMERICAN MANAGEMENT ASSOCIATION
New York ▪ Atlanta ▪ Brussels ▪ Chicago ▪ Mexico City
San Francisco ▪ Shanghai ▪ Tokyo ▪ Toronto ▪ Washington, D.C.

Bulk discounts available. For details visit:
www.amacombooks.org/go/specialsales
Or contact special sales:
Phone: 800-250-5308 / Email: specialsls@amanet.org
View all the AMACOM titles at: www.amacombooks.org
American Management Association: www.amanet.org

Library of Congress Cataloging-in-Publication Data

Geltman, Joani.
  A survival guide to parenting teens : talking to your kids about sexting, drinking, drugs, and other things that freak you out / Joani Geltman.
     pages cm
  ISBN-13: 978-0-8144-3366-9 (pbk.)
  ISBN-10: 0-8144-3366-9 (pbk.)
  1. Parent and teenager. 2. Parenting. I. Title.
  HQ799.15.G45 2014
  306.874—dc23
                                                            2013041885

About AMA

American Management Association (www.amanet.org) is a world leader in talent development, advancing the skills of individuals to drive business success. Our mission is to support the goals of individuals and organizations through a complete range of products and services, including classroom and virtual seminars, webcasts, webinars, podcasts, conferences, corporate and government solutions, business books, and research. AMA's approach to improving performance combines experiential learning—learning through doing—with opportunities for ongoing professional growth at every step of one's career journey.

Printing number
10 9 8 7 6 5

contents

foreword

I am not a perfect adult and I was not a perfect teen. Close. Perfect-ish.

I sometimes had an attitude, and frankly still do with my parents occasionally. I attribute this to knowing I am unconditionally loved by them, so it's okay to be my least charming self. (You're welcome Mom and Dad.) I procrastinated. I drank before I was 21. I threw horrible crying tantrums hating every piece of clothing I owned, leaving everything scattered on my floor at least a few times a week. I don't think I made my bed even once while I lived at home, and as you will read later in this book, I had a bit of a popsicle addiction, which included leaving the remaining sticks all over the house. But I am very pleased to report that as a 30-year-old woman, I've been almost entirely self-sufficient since I left home at 18, and I have a beautiful life that wouldn't have been possible without the emotional support of my parents. My bed gets made and my life is (more or less) in order. While there are no more popsicle sticks, there is usually one rogue pair of jeans on the floor that will never get put away, but guess what? Life goes on. Most importantly, even when I'm living 3,000 miles away, I still talk to my mom almost every day and get the majority of the most up-to-date news on my high school and college friends from her. I used to joke that my friends were only friends with me to get to Joani. As we're now all over 30 and she seems to see them more than I do, I wonder if this was really such a joke.

My mom didn't try to be "the cool mom." She was never more a friend than a parent, but her patience, understanding, and presence, practiced in all the ways she outlines in the book, have not only made me who I am today, but have created and sustained the most important relationship in my life—my relationship with her. This book is not about how she parented me (thank God). Her life's work has been to understand human beings and to help guide them. I only mention these things about where I am today as an individual and in relation to her, and her to my friends, as the truest indication and endorsement that she has practiced what she preaches. And I can confidently say I feel very good and grateful about where I am today.

I am firmly rooted in adulthood, but my teenage years don't feel so far away. With my hands outstretched, I can touch both sides. Being a teenager is so hard, and so is being an adult. The fact is, just being alive is hard. There is very little we have control over in this life, but my mother taught me I do have control over how I listen to other people and how to compassionately understand where someone is coming from. I learned this first and foremost by how she was with me. She is my survival guide. And now she gets to be yours.

Ari Graynor
(Daughter of Joani Geltman)

acknowledgments

To my agent, Lauren Galit, who first gave my unfocused but passionate book focus. Her commitment and belief in me were always unwavering.

To Bob Nirkind, who gave me this amazing publishing opportunity. His intuition about who I am and his guidance with what I wanted to accomplish with this book gave me great comfort as I plowed through this sometimes scary and intimidating, but amazingly fulfilling process.

To Louis Greenstein, my fantastic editor. Who knew editing could be so fun? His intelligence, humor, and total understanding of me—and my book—were priceless gifts.

To the hundreds of parents I have met over the years who laugh with me and cry with me. I admire their openness to parenting in a new way in this challenging new century, and their commitment and love for their children gives them the courage to change.

To my husband, Greg Graynor, who is always the first to encourage and champion any goal I set for myself.

To my daughter, Ari Graynor, who is my mentor and my inspiration. She shares her honesty, her experience, and her love for me in a way that nourishes me, supports me, and challenges me to be my best self.

introduction

HELP! I'M sick and tired of fighting with my teen about getting out of bed every morning!

Help! That attitude has to go! I've taken away the cellphone, the computer, and the Xbox, but he doesn't seem to care what he loses. He's still rude!

Help! My teen is on Facebook 24/7. Can't she just read a book for a change?

Help! I just picked up my teen's cellphone and OMG I can't believe what I read!

I get messages like these all the time from desperate parents anxious for answers to the daily hassles they experience with their teens. Which is why I wrote this book. When you're in a crisis with your teen—whether it's a blow-up between the two of you that got out of control; school, homework, and grades that have become a daily battle of wills; or frustration over your teen's cellphone addiction, Facebook use, or video games—you don't have the luxury of reading a tome on teen development. When you need help, you need help now! *A Survival Guide to Parenting Teens* is your 911 call. It's the "Hints from Heloise" of parenting books. You read what you need, when you need it.

This book contains 80 entries, grouped by categories ranging from keeping your teen motivated in school, to dealing with teen "attitude," to understanding your own parenting style, to social networking, to the classic teen triumvirate of sex, drugs, and alcohol. Each freestanding entry begins with a "Here's the Problem" section, which lays out a specific issue from your point of view.

The next section, "Why It's a Problem," explains what your teen was thinking . . . or not thinking. It provides you with an objective, "take your own emotions out of it for a minute" framework that offers you a perspective other than your own and can make all the difference when you're headlong into a crisis. Much of your interaction with your teen may feel very personal, but often it has nothing whatsoever to do with you. Nonetheless, when your teen pushes your buttons, it becomes all about you, which is the reason it's important to take a step back and understand the "why" of it all.

Finally, each entry ends with a "Here's the Solution" section that gives you a strategy. I tell you what to do, explain how to do it, and give you some ideas as to what to say to resolve the situation.

You can start anywhere. Whatever page you turn to, you now know exactly what you'll find in that entry: Here's what my teen's doing, here's why my teen's doing it, and here's what I can do to make it better. Ahhhh, you sigh, I think I can handle this!

I turned 60 recently . . . happily. This means I can now say I have literally spent more than half of my life working to become the parenting expert I am today. Times have changed, and the job of parenting has had to change a great deal in the past 30 years in response to the complexities of raising teens in this new century. As a therapist in private practice and as a therapist for teens in school settings, I once had the luxury of time to process and work through issues that parents and teens struggled with both individually and together. But in today's fast-paced world—with many parents working full-time in addition to raising families, and due to the many time-sensitive issues that crop up when you're raising a teen—there never seems to be enough time.

In response to the changing needs of families, I've had to totally change my model. Now I do parent coaching short term, and I do mean *short*. Most times I see parents for only one session. They tell me their problems, and I tell them what to do. That's my model: Give parents the information they need to understand their teen's behavior and offer them concrete strategies for intervention. *A Survival Guide to Parenting Teens* is your in-home version of my in-person coaching.

You are the first generation of parents whose experiences as teens don't match those of your kids'. In your own teen years, sex, drinking, and drugs were issues you faced firsthand. You can use this experience to guide your teens through these sometimes treacherous waters. But *your* teen years did not include computers, cellphones, texting and sexting, cyberbullying and cybersex, Facebook, and other social networking sites. For parents who did not experience these technologies as teens, this is a whole new frontier. Teens use and abuse technology. And parents may be completely unprepared to deal with it. The emotional and legal consequences are scary and the stakes are high.

Keep this book next to your bed, in your desk drawer at work, or in the glove compartment of your car. The next time you get an annoying text from your teen, or a call from a teacher at school concerned about your teen's missing homework, or an email from a parent reporting a weekend drinking escapade with a friend, pull out this book, get a plan, and exhale!

deflection and denial
your teen's main defense mechanisms

1

Here's the Problem

A mom called me recently for help. She described this situation: "My daughter comes in the door from school. I innocently say, 'Hi honey, how was your day?' I expect the usual grunt, but instead I'm bombarded by an avalanche of anger about issues that had nothing to do with school, ones that I thought had been resolved weeks before. And this all comes out of nowhere!" Baffled by this display of emotion, Mom gets hooked into the argument, a rehashing of old business. They both go to bed angry.

The next morning the daughter, sweet as pie, confesses to her mom that her grades were not as good as she thought they would be (report cards were in the mail). Mom congratulates her on her honesty.

Why It's a Problem

This teen came home from school with information she knew would be disappointing to her parents. The B she was expecting in English would now be a C. To preempt the "discussion" about the disappointing grade, the teen pulls a bait and switch: *I'll get mad at you before you get mad at me.* She starts in with some nonsensical argument to get the focus off the grade and onto something else less ego-deflating. She's using the art of deflection.

Teens use deflection and denial to avoid disappointing you, to avoid taking responsibility for behavior, and to protect themselves from their own feelings of shame. Defenses like these are problematic when they become a regular go-to response. Teaching teens to be honest with themselves and with others is a key to future healthy relationships. If your teen's diversion tactics can easily push your buttons, put you on the defensive, and avoid dealing with the real issue, then this may become her roadmap for life. Would you want to be married to that person?

Here's the Solution

This may be a look-in-the-mirror moment for a parent. Ask yourself: Do I put up barriers to truth telling? When my teen does something wrong or honestly admits to doing something wrong, do I immediately go to the "angry place"? Maybe this is the case, or maybe your teen just has a hard time seeing herself in a bad light, or doesn't want to be held responsible for bad choices. Either way, you need to communicate that it's all right to be imperfect and make mistakes.

When your teen leaves you scratching your head after a rant that comes from nowhere, this should be your clue that something else is going on. Rather than get hooked into an imaginary argument about nothing, you might say, "I get that you're angry about something, but I don't think it's this. If there's something you need to tell me about, and you're worried about how I'll respond, I understand. I promise I'll just listen and not react. I'm here for you, but I won't be drawn into an argument because you're upset or anxious about something else." At this point, with an "I love you" and a "let's talk later," I think you're done! Real arguments are hard enough, imaginary ones even harder!

2 my teenage clone
the power of conformity

Here's the Problem

I was visiting an all-girls middle and high school. At lunchtime, many of the girls were milling around the lobby where I sat. Glancing around, I noticed something striking: Literally, and I do mean literally, every single girl had a pair of UGG boots on her feet. For a second, I thought it might be part of the school uniform, but of course it wasn't. Moving up from their feet, I also noticed that almost every girl sported the same messy ponytail with a particular kind of barrette affixed somewhere on her head, no matter what length her hair. I was in a sea of clones!

It might not be UGG boots or ponytails for your teen, but a particular kind of jacket or backpack, sneakers or jeans, smartphone or iPad, that she must have or she'll "die." Maybe it's a TV show everyone watches and she needs to be able to participate in the teen version of the "water-cooler" discussion the morning after the show airs. Whatever the thing is, to your teen it's life or death!

Why It's a Problem

What's happened to your assertive, unique, and confident child? You know, the one who liked to dress a little quirky and loved reading instead of watching TV or tweeting away her time. Who's this child who could've cared less about label, brand, or style and now suddenly, that's *all* she cares about?

For most parents this "personality change" is a challenge. Teaching your children to think for themselves and not worry about what others think about them is a major parenting goal and life lesson. How reinforcing it's been over the years when they seem to have followed your advice. Until they don't! When they asked to buy an article of clothing, or go to a movie you didn't approve of, or wanted to listen to music that you knew was only because all the other kids were listening to it, you preached the "be yourself" sermon, and it worked like a charm. But now, suddenly, when you launch into that sermon, you get a "you just don't understand." You feel rejected, and your child feels judged. For the first time you feel worried that all the values you've worked so hard to develop in your child have vanished in the blink of an iPhone.

STOP WORRYING! All those values you've been promoting have not disappeared. They've only gone into hibernation for the next five to seven years. I promise, they're all still there. Part of raising teens is trusting that you've already done a wonderful job. Now it's their time to experience the world as they see it.

The culprit in this cloning behavior comes from new growth in the brain. Prior to adolescence, children define themselves by how they measure up. As nine- or ten-year-olds, they ran home after getting a 100 percent on a spelling test and couldn't wait to tell you, "I'm a smart person." Now as teens, new growth in the brain provides an additional level of awareness. It's not only how *they* see themselves—"I got an A on the midterm"—but also there's a new awareness of what *other* people are thinking about them: "I got an A on the midterm, and everybody thinks I'm a big nerd, or everyone thinks it's cool I'm so smart."

This hyper-sense of self-consciousness is now ever present. There's a constant worry that everyone is looking at them and judging them. If they don't wear the right clothes, have the same phone, listen to the same music, talk the same talk, then everyone—and I mean *everyone*—will think they're completely and utterly uncool.

This is where the clone-like behavior comes in. It's not a values issue, and it's not a character flaw in your children. It's developmentally normal! These new brains of theirs are just realizing that other people think things about them. Conformity and sameness give them a feeling of comfort at a time in their life when they feel the most emotionally vulnerable. "Looking and act-ing like everybody else means I'm one of them, I belong." As they begin to develop a sense of their own identity and confidence in their ability to make decisions for themselves, the need to conform fades away.

Here's the Solution

If you take the high road and continue to preach the "Why do you have to be like everyone else, just be yourself" sermon, your teen will feel judged and criticized. She'll fear she is not good enough for you. This doesn't mean that you don't have a say. When she comes to you with a request that you know is because "all the other kids . . . ," here's what you can do. If it's unsafe, or unreasonable, say, "I get how important this is to you, and I know all your friends have it/are doing it. I know that not having/doing it will make you feel different from your friends, and I'm really sorry about that. I know how that feels, but it just isn't safe and I'm willing to take the heat from you to make sure you are safe." Understanding goes a lot further than judging.

Maybe she wants something that all her friends have that costs a ridicu-lous amount of money, and you feel strongly that it's a stupid thing to buy. Rather than accusing her of being stupid, which is how she will hear your "no," you can say, "I get how important it is for you to have this. It seems like a lot of money to me, so here's what I'm willing to do. I'll give you X amount of money, and you can pay the rest with your own money." You're modeling your values about money without judging or criticizing your teen.

Adolescence is the time when you and your teen will start to part ways in many areas. Sometimes teens adopt a new style of dress, new ideas about pol-itics or religion, and behaviors and personality traits that seem foreign to you and that are very different from yours. That's a good thing. That means they are taking the "growing-up" thing seriously.

So relax, all is not lost because they want to look like every other kid on the block. *You* know they're special and unique and that's all that matters.

3

getting your teen up in the morning
strategies for eliminating the daily fight from the morning routine

Here's the Problem

I'm guessing that like most parents you harbor sweet memories of early-morning rituals with your four-year-old, now a teenager. Mornings used to be full of cuddling, making goo-goo eyes, and whispering "I love you" in each other's ears. Now, "I love you" becomes "I hate you, leave me alone!" as you cajole, then nudge, then outright scream for your teen to get out of his damn bed!

I work with many parents who complain that their entire day is ruined by the early-morning battles with their teens to get them up for school. Their teen eventually gets up and gets out the door, none the worse for wear. But it's the parents who are left with the "battle scars," missing their train into the city and being late for work . . . again, making their other children late for school . . . again, running out to the car pool driver and apologizing for their teen's lateness . . . again, and the worst, spending the entire day with knots in their stomachs after another morning of screaming and yelling. This is no way to live.

If you are a parent who looks toward your teen's future, then solving the wake-up problem should be very important to you. My college students cite this as *the hardest* task as a freshman—getting up and getting to class on time. Those students whose parents took on the onus for getting them up and out are at a complete loss when they get to college. They haven't developed their own strategies for taking on this responsibility. This is something you need to start now.

Why It's a Problem

As teens enter puberty, their biological or circadian clocks set themselves back a few hours, preparing for the longer days of adulthood and the need for less sleep. This means that their bodies and minds might not be *ready* for sleep until 11 p.m. Here's the kicker: Though their minds and bodies say, "Stay awake," that one foot still in childhood is saying, "You need nine hours of sleep a night for the brain to do all its work." Therein lies the contradiction. We see how exhausted and out of sorts they are in the morning, and we know that if they would just go to bed earlier, this whole problem would be solved. Ah, if it were only that easy.

Many parents still try to enforce a bedtime and require their teens to be in bed by 9:30, knowing that will get them the required nine hours. This sensible bedtime can actually be the culprit. Remember that a waking-up issue is directly related to a falling-asleep issue. If the brain isn't ready to shut down at 9:30, then this too-early bedtime can send them into presleep anxiety, worried they will be unable to fall asleep. And of course, that becomes a self-fulfilling prophecy.

Another cause of sleeping and waking issues is that teen brains can be overstimulated before bed; cellphones, laptops, and iPads used in bed give the brain a mixed message. Using those devices requires an active brain. To sleep, you need a quiet brain.

Here's the Solution

In order to know how to work on the "getting up," you need to look at the "going to sleep." For one week, observe the evening habits of your teen. Stay up as late as he does. What's he doing an hour before he shuts off the lights? Is he texting in bed, on Facebook, or playing video games? Check your phone records. Is there texting after lights out? During this weeklong observation period, refrain from commenting or giving advice; this is just a time to take notes. Also, keep tabs on the morning wake-up ritual. How many times did you need to give the wake-up nudge? How long exactly did the whole process take from initially entering his room, to getting him dressed, fed, and out the door?

Now at least you have some data and hopefully some proof positive that something your teen is doing before bed is affecting his ability to start the day with a smile—if only! Next, share this research with your teen. The conversation will go like this: "Over the past week, I've noticed that you're up quite late, texting and on Facebook or playing games on your computer or phone. I get how important that is to you. I've also noticed that staying up past 11 makes it that much harder for you to get up in the morning, and that's become a problem for both of us." Present your data. This is an important piece. Your teen is not at all motivated to change what he's doing and will most likely say that none of this is a problem.

At this point it's time for you and your teen to come up with a plan that addresses your research. Come up with a time when all electronics "leave the building." Ideally this would be 30 to 60 minutes before bedtime. Remember, these devices belong to you. If your teen "chooses" to fight you on this, then you can "choose" to get rid of them altogether. TV and music are exempt. These are more passive activities that often provide a calming influence.

That's the going to sleep part. Now we get to the waking up. Most important, you need to let your teen know what you're willing to do to help and what you're no longer willing to do. Set whatever limits feel right for you. Perhaps you're willing to do an initial wake-up before you go downstairs, and then maybe come up *once* for a second wake-up call. What you should not be willing to do is take abuse or make it your life's work to get your teen out of bed in the morning. This is something that is extremely important to impart to your teen. This conversation should always start with "I get how hard it is getting up in the morning. School starts early and you're not a morning person. But we need to find something that works, because I won't be fighting you on this every morning. Those days are over, so we need to work this out."

Perhaps some kind of incentive might help. Everyone needs motivation, and getting up and going to school is not motivating. Maybe for every morning your teen gets up without fighting, you'll pay to download music. Or maybe he starts with a kitty of $25 for weekend spending money. For every morning he doesn't get up on time you deduct $5. If the weekend comes and he has no money, so be it! If you have a girl, maybe reward her with a Friday afternoon manicure or pedicure for a week of waking up on time.

You and your teen should come up with an action plan that includes wake-up calls, alarm clocks, your texts from the kitchen, or hiring a mariachi band to play under his window (just kidding about the mariachi band). If he misses the bus or car pool, or you need to leave, there's no ride from you. If that results in detention for being late to school, that's life! Teens need to feel the consequences of their actions. They may have to walk or call a cab. But do not rescue!

Relationships are reciprocal. If the morning has gone badly and your teen has been particularly angry and abusive, then later in the day when he comes to you for rides, money, laundry, etc., a calm "I would, I love doing things for you, but your lack of effort this morning on getting up and out has made it impossible for me to do that for you today. Let's try again tomorrow." For tomorrow is another day!

4 you can't always get what you want
the demanding and entitled teen

Here's the Problem

Your teen walks into the kitchen while you're preparing dinner and says, "I need to go to Staples" or "All my jeans are dirty and I need you to do my laundry" or "I'm going to Dan's house and I need a ride," etc. From a teen's point of view, needs and wants take precedence over anything of importance that you might be doing. God forbid you have something else to do and you politely say, "Honey I can't, I have to [fill in the blank]."

Perhaps your teen makes a demand and you get aggravated. How dare she think that you will just be at her beck and call! You say as much, and an argument follows, with your teen not getting at all why you're so aggravated. After all, isn't on-demand parenting your job?

Why It's a Problem

During adolescence, teens by nature, biologically speaking, are self-centered and narcissistic. They are often completely unaware of someone else's perspective. Their growing brains are filled with thoughts, worries, and desires that are new to them. Consequently, just managing and keeping up with that deluge is a full-time job, making them impervious to other points of view. This doesn't mean they are necessarily bratty, spoiled, or entitled. You may in fact have a spoiled, bratty, entitled teen, but that can also be a result of overindulgence, not biology. I am talking about your normal, run-of-the-mill, demanding teen. They just need to be taught to slow down and ask a question rather than making a statement of want.

You don't need to rebuke; you need to retrain.

Here's the Solution

Every time your teen comes to you with "I need you to . . ." or "I want you to . . ." or "You have to . . ." you can calmly say, "Is there a question in there?" No giving answers until the demand is put in the form of a question. This gives you the opportunity to agree or not, based on your availability and your desire.

Everybody deserves the respect of choice. This includes your teen. Rather than demanding that he help you, why not model the behavior you want from him? Instead of "Take out the trash . . . now!" or "Shut off the computer and do your homework!" try "Honey, I could use some help with the trash. Can you help me?" or "Honey, can we come up with a time you'll get off the computer and do your homework?" You'll still get resistance, but it will serve a greater goal. There's nothing more fun for a teen than to catch his parent being a hypocrite. At least now when your teen demands something from you and you tell him you won't respond to demands, he can't throw this in your face: "Well, you just demand things of me. You never ask me nicely. Why should I have to ask you nicely?"

If you can see this as a teaching moment, like teaching your toddler to say please and thank you, you'll be on easy street. It will make you like your teen a lot more. And remember, practice makes perfect. This might take a while.

5 too much time on their hands
the busier the teen, the more motivated

Here's the Problem

Not all teens have busy lives. Some go to school, come home, get on the computer, go to their video games, and settle in for the rest of the day and night. For these teens, the rest of the day and night can be a full day's worth of hanging out if you add up the hours. Most high schools are done by 2:30 p.m., bus ride 30 minutes, and then home by 3:00 p.m. That leaves a full eight hours of screen time or other time-wasting pursuits before bed. Not good. If teens with this kind of time on their hands don't use it for studying and reading *War and Peace*, there's a problem. It brings to mind the old adage, "The more time you have, the less you do."

Why It's a Problem

Teens who have this amount of unstructured time tend to be teens whose school motivation is low. Self-esteem comes from being active, involved, and feeling that you've accomplished something at the end of the day. This makes the next day something to look forward to. For kids who haven't found their niche in sports, or activities in or out of school, every day becomes a repeat of the day before, with little to look forward to and little to feel good about. When you feel good and motivated about a job, a sport, music, or drama, then those feelings often bridge to less motivating or fulfilling parts of your life, like school.

Your teen is in the beginning stages of developing an identity. *Who am I? What turns me on? What makes me happy?* Many teens are overwhelmed by the choices and have absolutely no idea how to get off that couch or away from the computer screen. Too many options confuse them, so they choose the familiar and comfortable. They need you to understand that, not to judge them as lazy sloths. Teens need incentives. For some, the roar of the crowd during a football game, acting in the school play, or getting a paycheck from a part-time job is their incentive.

Here's the Solution

There are many teens who actually have a passion or a talent but have no idea how it might translate to the real world. Perhaps your teen loves photography and is always taking pictures of family, friends, and pets. He may be too shy or lack the confidence to seek out the school newspaper or yearbook office and offer to be a staff photographer. Or maybe your teen is a great artist but would never think about being the scenic designer for the school play. You may need to do a little undercover work by seeking out the faculty adviser for that particular area. Let this person know that your teen has a lot of talent in this area but is too shy to get involved. Ask if the adviser might be willing to personally invite your teen to participate. Many teens are paralyzed with self-consciousness and need the help of a caring adult.

Money is always a great motivator. You could say to your couch potato: "We think it's really important for you to find something to do after school. We've noticed that having so much time on your hands isn't really helpful to you. You aren't using the time for homework or even hanging with friends, and too much screen time can affect your motivation for doing things that are good for you. We'd like to see you look for a part-time job or for a volunteer or internship position. If you choose not to do this, then we choose not to just give you spending money. We'll be happy to pay you for work you can do around the house in lieu of a job, or we'll help you find a job. You can also do a sport or an activity at school or go to the gym regularly. You have a ton of options. If you're busy doing something positive, then we'll be happy to give you money or buy you what you want or need. I get that you like and need a lot of downtime. And we're OK with a few hours of that, but not from 3 to 11 p.m. every day. So let's do some planning."

the power of puberty
changing body, changing brain

Here's the Problem

A dad called me for coaching. He was worried about his 16-year-old son, who seemed depressed and angry all the time. The dad was puzzled, because his son was smart, did well in school, and was an extremely talented athlete. He was on two varsity teams even though he was only a sophomore. How, he wondered, could a boy with so much success be so miserable? The dad gave me another piece of the puzzle. It seems that since his son entered puberty he's been plagued with terrible acne.

His father described this scene at one of his son's lacrosse games: His son would go onto the field and make an amazing play. As soon as he came back to the bench, he sat at the farthest end away from his teammates with the hood of his sweatshirt pulled up as far as possible to shield his face. When his teammates wanted to high-five him he'd nod his head and avoid making eye contact.

Why It's a Problem

Puberty can be devastatingly awful. It's a cruel twist of fate that just as a teen is at the height of self-consciousness, his body turns on him. Perhaps your son also has bad acne, or maybe your daughter is flat-chested. Maybe your son is the shortest in his class, or maybe as a fifth grader he is the tallest, with facial hair to boot. Whatever it is, no matter how insignificant it may seem to you, it's a big deal to them.

Adding fuel to the fire is that teens can be extremely cruel to each other. Making fun of someone else's vulnerabilities makes their own seem less awful. Talk about a double whammy. "I hate that I'm flat-chested, and now my friends call me 'little boy.'"

What makes this a hard issue for parents is that your teen is probably not walking around the house saying, "I hate this about my body." Instead what happens is a meltdown two minutes before leaving for school. "I have nothing to wear; you never buy me any clothes. I told you those jeans make me look fat; why did you let me buy them?" And because your teen's ride is sitting in front of your house, or the bus is at the bus stop, you have your own meltdown. You scream, "You ungrateful spoiled brat, what do you mean I never buy you clothes? I just spent $200 on clothes for you!"

The truth is, it isn't about the jeans. In that two minutes before she was about to leave, she looked in the mirror and someone looked back that made her feel ill. It's really that simple. If you pay too much attention to the tantrum's content, you'll miss the real story.

Here's the Solution

Understanding is your greatest weapon against puberty. You can't change your teen's genes, and you can't "make this all better." It's nature. Be careful not to minimize the impact of puberty. When your teen complains about being fat or ugly, pimply, too tall or too short, try hard not to go for the "But honey, you're beautiful" or "You're handsome." It will feel disingenuous to your teen, because that's absolutely not how he or she feels. Better to say, "I am so sorry you feel that way, you know I don't see you that way at all, but I get that you feel that."

The next time your teen throws a tantrum before school, before a school dance, or before leaving the house on a Friday night to hang out with friends, remember that for teenagers to put themselves and their bodies on public display during this difficult stage is hard. Rather than joining in the argument and becoming the scapegoat for all that is wrong with your teen's body, you can hug your teen and say, "I get that you're not feeling good about how you look. Is there anything I can do to help?" It won't make the acne go away or make the boobs a more preferred size or make him six feet tall, but at least someone "gets" that life just sucks sometimes!

And please, no teasing. I know Uncle Harry thinks it's funny to call your short-for-his-age 15-year-old "shrimp," but it's not! And you can let Uncle Harry know.

7 L is for lazy

getting your teens to do what you want them to do

Here's the Problem

When my daughter was a teen it was Popsicle sticks. On the arm of the couch, under the couch, in between the cushions of the couch, on her desk. The invasion lasted for six years. I am happy to report that as a young adult she knows how to throw her trash away and takes pride in maintaining a lovely living space. In fact, when I'm staying with her, I'm put on notice to keep it neat!

For you, it may be returning clean laundry to your teen's room and still seeing it sitting there in the basket days later, now covered with dirty laundry. Maybe it's getting your teen to take out the trash in time for pickup or getting him to clean up food wrappers and dirty dishes off his bedroom floor. When it comes to lazy teens, all parents have their crosses to bear.

Why It's a Problem

This is a universal plight for parents of teenagers. Teens subscribe to the "eat, drink, and leave" principle and the "I'll do it, just leave me alone!" technique. I don't see it as laziness, but distraction. Here's the progression: "I'm hungry/thirsty; I think I'll have a _____." The consuming of the snack commences. This is followed by the putting down of the glass, plate, or wrapping on the floor, windowsill, or couch cushion so he can continue to engage in the more interesting aspects of his life like napping, texting, or Facebook. It's not a matter of deliberately avoiding responsibility; it's just a complete lack of interest.

The biggest hurdle is differing expectations. For parents, being responsible to their family and home is their highest priority. For teens, it's the lowest, at least for now. Their primary interests are themselves and their friends. Everything else plays second fiddle. Thank you, teenage narcissism.

Here's the Solution

Option 1: As I think back to the Popsicle-stick conundrum, I realize I never had a wastebasket in the TV room. Maybe if I had put a basket literally right next to the couch on the side she always sat on, she probably would have used it. My bad! Your first option is to see if there is a solution other than yelling at them to clean up after themselves. Think like a design consultant and engage your teen in the process with you. Your conversation might start: "I get that when you're finished with your soda/snack/juice you just put it down while you get on with something else and then forget about it. But it's making me crazy, and we're getting ants/flies as a result. Other than me yelling, let's come up with a solution." Teens are smart about this kind of stuff.

Option 2: You give the reminder, "Hey honey, don't forget to throw away your X" or "Trash day is tomorrow, you need to take out the trash tonight." Expect that the first reminder will go unheeded. Decide beforehand the number of times you're willing to give the reminder. I think three is a fair number. When your teen doesn't do X after the third reminder, don't say another word! If the chore is time-sensitive, do it yourself. If it's something that hasn't been cleaned up, leave it there. The next time that day, or the next day, that your teen asks you for a ride, money, laundry, snack, help with homework, etc., you say calmly and without sarcasm and anger: "I'd love to. Let me know when you have thrown away your wrapper and brought your dirty glass/plate into the kitchen, and I will be glad to help you/give you/take you/buy you. . . ." Or "Since you made a choice not to take out the trash, I'm making a choice to not do X."

Yelling and labeling your teen as lazy will not engender cooperation, just attitude. Helping him or her to understand that relationships are reciprocal is more meaningful.

Option 3: Just do it yourself. You have bigger fish to fry. Chalk it up to normal teen behavior. Know that as they get older and live on their own, and the parent maid service no longer exists, they'll figure it out. It's just a moment in time. They have a lot on their minds, and wrappers/plates and glasses just do not take up any space in their overloaded brain. For you, this can take up a lot of negative energy. Why not give yourself some peace?

8

trust vs. temptation

how to help a sneaky teen

Here's the Problem

A parent called me to ask, "What do you do when your teen betrays your trust? Can and how do you rebuild it?" Trust is a tricky issue with teens. An adult perspective is that someone earns your trust by showing through their behavior that they understand and respect your expectations. Because adults have more life experience and the ability to think things through, it's realistic to expect that when adults betray your trust, they fully understand what they're doing. A cognitive choice has been made: *I know I'm not supposed to be doing this, and I am doing it anyway.*

Why It's a Problem

Of course teens can think, but they don't often think things through. It's their spontaneity and impulsivity that drives their behavior. In other words, they may *feel* more than they think. The "excitement" of it all is very powerful. At the moment when "awesome" comes around, it may be in direct conflict with a rule or expectation that you have of them. For example, your teen has promised you that she'll never go to a party where no parents are present. You find out that she lied and went to an unsupervised party. You could characterize this as a betrayal of trust. Or you could explain her "betrayal" another way. She and her friends drive up to the party. Your teen asks her friend, "Do you think the parents are home?" She replies, "Are you kidding? No way!" Now your teen has a dilemma. She knows she's not supposed to go into this house without parents, yet she watches as so many kids walk in looking care-free and conflict-free about their decision. She knows on the one hand that she is not supposed to (trust issue), but she wants to so badly because every-one else is (temptation issue). She'll look like a loser if she says no (hyper-self-consciousness). The cute boy she has a crush on is inside (temptation issue). She feels like she looks really cute (has on a good outfit). Oh, what's a girl to do? She goes in! I would see this as a temptation issue, not a trust issue. Imagine how hard it is to walk away from all that "awesomeness."

Here's the Solution

Rather than going to the "you've betrayed my trust; you lied; you're grounded" place, you could say something like this: "I found out that the parents weren't home. I thought we had an understanding that you're not to go into a house without parents. On the other hand, I get how hard it must be when you're actually in the car, in front of the house, and desperate to go in. I know you want to do the right thing. But it must be really hard when you see all your friends going in, to just walk away. We need to figure out a plan so that the next time you're in this situation, you'll have another option rather than lying. Maybe you can call me and let me know the parents aren't home. If things have been going well with us, maybe I will let you stay for a few minutes so you can say hi to your friends and see that cute boy you have a crush on. Then you can feign illness or an early morning family gathering and slip out the door, and I'll pick you up around the corner. That way you get to save face, stay safe, and not lie."

It's important for parents to recognize the "power of the moment." It's unrealistic to expect that a teen, full of impulse and excitement, will always be able to do the right thing and exercise self-control. Many adults find that hard. If your teen feels she can call you for help and "trusts" that you won't yell, you may be able to bypass the lying and the sneakiness. Encourage honesty by offering help.

9 lies of omission
"oh. I didn't think
I had to tell you that"

Here's the Problem

Sometimes people lie outright, and sometimes they just don't tell you the whole story. Why do teens lie? They lie because from their point of view, they have to. How else do they get to do what they want? The problem is that they don't even give their parents a chance to say yes. Instead they tell half the story. Because teens are impulsive and live in the moment, they often get caught. The best way to cure this? Your teen needs to know that you won't always be the parent of no. Sometimes as parents you do resort to the knee-jerk no because your teen demands rather than asks, and that ticks you off. Sometimes they catch you when you're busy, and just to shoo the issue away you say no. Maybe in the past, they asked permission to do something similar and you said no, so now they know not to ask but to just do.

Why It's a Problem

Here are a couple of cases in point: A 13-year-old girl has her parents drop her off in front of a school where she tells them she'll be attending a sports event. Instead, she meets up with a few friends there, and they walk into town to meet a group of boys. When the mom calls the parent who is supposed to pick up the girls, he tells her that his daughter never went to the school. He dropped her off in town and that's where he's picking the girls up at the appointed hour. What a silly lie. When confronted by the mom, the girl says she assumed her mom would have said no to letting her walk around town. She then says, "I did go to the game [even though it was only for five seconds] so I didn't lie. I just didn't tell you I was going into town."

Another story: A 15-year-old girl who lives 30 minutes by train outside of New York City tells her parents she's going to sleep over at so-and-so's house. When her parents drop her off, the friend's parents are home and all appears to be well. Then Mom finds out from a friend who was heading back from the city at 10 p.m. that she'd seen her daughter on the same train. Whaaaatttt? The mother explains that her daughter knows she isn't allowed to go into the city at night without adult supervision. Apparently the sleep-over house parent, who drove the girls to the train station and picked the girls up there at 10:30 p.m., never questioned this girl as to whether her parents had given her permission to go into the city at night on the train, and the girl never said anything about it.

Here's the Solution

These girls never gave their parents a chance to discuss their wishes, and now they have to deal with the consequences of lying. That's the teen's feeling brain for you. The impulsive need to go and do is so strong that it overwhelms rational thinking. And that's the point. In both of these cases there was room for a non-no answer. It's true that in the past these parents had said no to similar requests, and the girls felt they had no other choice. Your job is to help your kids come up with a plan that could possibly make it a yes. For example, with the New York City girl, a compromise might have been reached along the lines of "I get that you really want to go into the city alone with your friends. I don't feel safe having you go in at night, but you could go late in the afternoon, and take a train home at 7:30 or 8:00 and still have time to get dinner and walk around in the early evening." I'm guessing that would have been an OK compromise. In the walking-into-town case, the girl knew that her mom was uncomfortable with the kids rambling around town. Mom and daughter could have come up with a plan together that would have made Mom comfortable. Instead of an open-ended hang with friends in the park or downtown, put a mutually agreed-upon amount of time on the hanging part of the activity. Some time is *always better* than no time! Make sure there are hourly check-ins and location change notifications.

Your job is to say to your kids, "Give us a chance. Maybe we can find a way to make it happen for you that feels good to both of us. Don't give us that chance and you might get caught in your lie and end up with a consequence that is unpleasant. I know we sometimes say no without thinking. We'll work on that so you don't need to lie."

Remember, helping your kids come up with a plan that works for both of you is so much better and more pleasant than sitting home with a grounded teen. Nobody wants to do that!

10 why don't boys talk?
a different kind of silent treatment

Here's the Problem

A parent at her wit's end, who couldn't get her teen son to talk to her, came to me for help. She could see and sense that all was not well with him; he looked unhappy, seemed lonely, and isolated himself in his room. This was not an intentional silent treatment, the mom explained. There had been no arguments, punishments, or incidents of wrongdoing. He was completely shut down, and this mom was worried.

Why It's a Problem

I asked the mom to describe her husband's personality and how he dealt with uncomfortable feelings. I wanted to find out what kind of model this boy had grown up with. She said that he was a quiet guy who kept his feelings to himself. Turns out that the dad and his son had a lot in common. Mom also seemed unbearably uncomfortable and in unfamiliar territory as she haltingly shared her story. This was a woman who normally kept things to herself, but she could see her son was in pain and wanted desperately to help him, even if it meant going out of her own comfort zone.

There are three things at play here. First, this 14-year-old boy is experiencing the world in a new way. He's probably uncomfortable with his new body, his new brain, and all the normal angst of adolescence. He may be in the middle of a transition time with old friends, some moving on to other people, leaving him with a void and no idea how to fill it. If he were a teen girl, it might be easier to deal with all these new feelings. Boys and girls, men and women, are different. Period. Our bodies are different, our brains and driving hormones are different, and our culture raises us differently. A girl may cry, talk to her friends, and be entirely comfortable expressing her feelings to anyone willing to listen. Not so much for teen boys.

Second, if he's a shy guy, then his personality style is in this mix. You have a boy feeling all kinds of things he's never felt before and no comfortable outlet to express them. Finally, if this is a family in which people keep their feelings mostly to themselves, this boy might not have the feeling language to communicate what's going on with him.

Here's the Solution

If your kid jumped out into the middle of the street and you saw a car coming, instinctively you would jump in to save him. In adolescence, your teen is jumping into the street on a regular basis, and you need to have a huge repertoire of life-saving techniques. An important one may be to look at your own behavior, personality, and attitudes and evaluate the model you've presented to your kids about how to handle life's ups and downs. In this family, the boy might not have been given the tools to unravel his own feelings. Instead he's following the family legacy of shutting down and keeping those things locked up inside. How wonderful it would be for the dad to say to his son: "You know I'm not very good at this feeling thing. I know I don't talk much at all about what's going on with me, and like you, I didn't talk at all to my parents. But I can see that you have a lot on your mind. I know what that feels like. I remember when I was your age (share some stories, insights). I get that talking to your mom and me might feel uncomfortable, because I feel like that a lot, even now as an adult. But I love you, and we can work on this together." Insert your observations such as "I notice you don't seem to be hanging with so-and-so anymore" or "You used to love playing soccer. It feels like something has changed for you." Rather than asking questions, try to make observations of changes you have noticed. Sometimes that can help open him up.

Raising a teen requires parents to take a good hard look at their own lives. Your teen's level of awareness of who you are and how you handle the storms and stresses of life has never been more important. This can be a time for enormous new growth for you. A good therapist costs a ton of money. Let your teen do it for free!

11 my kid the quitter
why won't my teen stick with anything?

Here's the Problem

With much enthusiasm, your teen signs up for a sport, a musical instrument, or an after-school club. Halfway into the season, lessons, or semester she tells you she wants to quit. Sound familiar? I'm guessing you have a number of rental agreements for the trumpets or clarinets now gathering dust in the hall closet, or expensive must-have sports equipment abandoned in the basement. On the one hand, you're disappointed in your teen: "She never finishes anything; she has no passion. I don't want her to learn that if you don't like something, you can just quit it. I hate that she's letting the team down by quitting midseason." On the other hand, you might think that if your teen says she wants to quit, there is really nothing you can do about it. Either way it just feels bad. You don't want your teen to be that "quitter kid."

Why It's a Problem

Teens in particular are well-known for being "quitters." The most important thing in your teen's life is her friends. If most of her friends are into a sport or band or the school play, then that's what she'll want to be into too, regardless of whether she likes it or has any talent or interest in it. The coaches/directors/faculty advisers, on the other hand, think that kids who join their team/play/club are interested in it and are motivated to do the best they can. If your teen joined because that's what her friends are doing, she's probably more interested in sitting on the bench and yammering away with friends than actually playing the sport. This will definitely tick off the coaches, who might not be win-focused but at least want their team members to put their fullest effort into the practices and games. This is when the discontent begins.

A teen joins a team to hang with friends. The coach sees this teen chatting and fooling around and not paying attention during practice. At first the coach may say in a mildly irritated voice, "Hey guys, pay attention." Then when that doesn't seem to stop the stem of chatter, he may disapprove more loudly with something stronger and perhaps meaner. Then at game time, he could further punish this distracting player by keeping her on the bench. For this teen, the fun factor of being with friends has diminished. Now it's just another place to get hassled by an adult. Additionally, her friends may be seriously into this sport/play/club and do not want to chat and fool around. It's at this moment your teen may say, "I quit." It's become a lose-lose activity. Friends aren't any fun, and the coaches are mean. Not fun, all done!

Another cause for quitting may be that your teen actually was interested in playing this sport but is not very good at it. Since self-consciousness is at an all-time high in adolescence, your teen may be feeling a heightened sense of humiliation. Perhaps when she gets on the field, she drops the ball, misses the ball, loses the ball, or sends it places where no one can field it. Or perhaps she's a slow runner. Coaches may give "feedback" to your teen in front of her friends, and the result is that she ends up on the bench during games and leaves feeling humiliated and dejected. One parent told me, "The coaches have been very discouraging. They *tell* her to quit." Doesn't sound like much fun to me.

In either scenario, your teen is miserable. When she joined up she had expectations that have not been realized. Your teen is at the buffet of life, exploring all kinds of new foods. Sometimes the ones she thought she'd love turn out to be "yucky," and sometimes they become new favorites. There's really no predicting here. There are so many variables in play that motivate your teen to try new things. *What do my friends like? What am I good at? What is fun and exciting? What do my parents expect of me? What's valued to be good at in my community?* Sometimes, these motivations are at odds with one another, and teenagers don't always have the experience or ability to think rationally and to play out the consequences of their decisions.

Here's the Solution

When your teen comes to you and says, "I quit," here are some strategies: First, if your child is a younger teen, I would put a call in to the coach/teacher/director and say, "My son wants to quit X. I'm wondering if you can help me understand what might be going on, and if you have any suggestions. Finishing something you start is important to us, and if he quits I want to make sure he understands why and what the consequences are." I would then go back to your teen with the information you got from this person and discuss it. Sometimes kids just need a little prodding, and he will give it another shot after some strategizing. You might say, "I get that you're unhappy with X, and it's just not fun anymore. Tell me some of the things that you hate about it. Can you think of anything you could do to make it better? If you do choose to quit, you'll need to call the coach/teacher/director and tell him yourself. You can't just stop going; you need to take responsibility for your decision. Let's talk about what you will say to him." At the least, your teen will learn that sometimes quitting something is just as hard as sticking with it.

Your teen may be making the right decision; sucking it up isn't always character building, especially if one's self-esteem takes a beating. So the next time your teen wants to "join up," make sure that you have a discussion that helps him think through his decision. Teens are impulsive, irrational, and emotional, which leads to decisions that often backfire. Finding interests that we love and to which we can commit is a lifelong pursuit. Be patient with the process.

12 the parent-teen power struggle
you can't make me

Here's the Problem

When your children are young, they're your most enthusiastic supporters. Sharing and introducing them to your passions and interests is one of the greatest joys of parenthood. For one mother and father who sought me out, the passion was skiing. In past years, the family of four had equally enjoyed this activity so much that this year they decided to rent a ski house for the season. This is no small expense and the parents hoped that this would be a great opportunity for family time, chatting in line and on the lifts, skiing the trails together, etc.

Seemingly out of nowhere, however, their 12-year-old daughter, a previously enthusiastic skier, now only wants to sit in the lodge and "veg." The parents, feeling helpless and angry, have this conversation with her, which I'm sure will be familiar to many of you.

"Do you want to have a friend up?" they ask.

"No."

"Do you want to stay home with a friend this weekend?"

"No."

"Well, you can't just stay home and do nothing."

"I know."

"What do you want to do?"

"I don't know."

Crying ensues.

Why It's a Problem

This girl is feeling differently about skiing this season, and her parents are deeply disappointed and frustrated. Maybe she's self-conscious in a way she never felt before. Maybe she doesn't like the way she looks in her ski clothes. Maybe as her body is changing she feels awkward and uncoordinated. Maybe she doesn't really like skiing; it was always her parents' thing, and now that she has this new brain, she's realizing she did it to make them happy. Maybe, maybe, maybe, it could be a thousand things that she can't articulate. It just doesn't feel right.

Along with embarrassment and worry about how others see them, teens also come to understand that parents really can't *make* them do whatever they want them to do anymore. For parents of teenagers, this can be a rude awakening. A "Just do it" no longer works, and there are no more "time-outs." When a teen digs his heels in, watch out! You can't talk him out of it and you can't punish or threaten him out of it either. Whatever is behind these powerful feelings, teens will fight back, feeling that the alternative (what parents want them to do) is way worse than whatever punishment the parents may choose to dole out. The other frustration for parents is, like the 12-year-old in the story, most kids can't articulate what exactly is going on; they just know what they know. Something feels really, really bad, and they will stand their ground to avoid feeling worse, no matter what the consequences. This is beyond frustrating for parents, who are determined to figure out the problem and fix it. The good news is that this is just a moment in time, maybe a few years, and as they gain some confidence and self-understanding this becomes at least a conversation rather than an inquisition.

Here's the Solution

For this skiing family the parents began to understand that their daughter needed and wanted to make her own decision about skiing. They were able to reframe their own disappointment into understanding and acceptance: "She's not lazy, she's an excellent student, and she wants to be with us (thankfully). She just doesn't want to ski. Maybe sometimes she just needs to sit in the lodge with her music, or a book, and be very content. And *we* need to be OK with that, too. She's such a wonderful girl. We just want her to be happy, but this is all part of growing up and learning who she is, trials and triumphs."

It's a normal part of development for teens to want to take on more control over their lives, but it's sometimes hard for parents to give it up.

13

helping your teen with remembering

you forgot your _____ again?

Here's the Problem

You've reminded your son or daughter at least 10 times in the last 24 hours not to forget his or her (fill in the blank). You know, whatever that thing is: books, sports equipment, permission slip, lunch, etc. etc. etc. This is now becoming a daily ritual. You say, "Don't forget," and they say with increasing frustration, "I won't!" It's as if they've never forgotten anything in their lives. And then of course there's the phone call from school or from practice: "Hiiiii," said in the sweetest and most loving voice you've ever heard from your teen, and then the dreaded words, "I FORGOT MY _____ ."

Naturally, it's at the most inopportune time. You're just about to walk out the door or go into a meeting or are dripping wet from the shower, and you lose it. "How many times did I ask you if you had your _____? That's it. I'm done. I've had it! No way! OK, where do I bring it?" You cave! Why? Because even though your teen hasn't thought ahead of the consequences, you have. The teacher said he would give your kid a zero if he forgot his book again; the coach said your kid would be benched if he forgot his equipment again; and so on and so on. So you leave whatever you're doing so that your kid doesn't get penalized for forgetting. But how will your teen ever learn to remember?

Why It's a Problem

This is like watching a rerun of your least favorite show when there's nothing else on TV. It's torture. If it makes you feel any better, all teens are forgetful. It's not just your teen. It's a normal consequence of an overloaded brain. When you yelled up the stairs the night before or in the morning before school, your teen registered it for a second, and that's when you got the scream, "I have it!" But seconds later, she receives a text from a friend asking some really important question like, "What are you wearing today?" Or just before getting organized to come downstairs, she looked in the mirror and was disgusted by what she saw, or her favorite song just played on her iPod shuffle, and whatever she was supposed to remember has been supplanted by something else. Teens are driven to distraction. Their brains deliver so many new thoughts every moment that it is almost impossible for them to keep track. Just telling them to remember does not work. It does in the moment you scream, and then it gets lost in the hurricane-force wind that is their thinking.

Here's the Solution

The work is to help them come up with a strategy for remembering. The key in designing this strategy is that it has to be something that works for who they are and how their brains work. Maybe you're a list maker, and if you could just get your teen to make a list the night before of what he has to do, and what he must remember for the next day, your life would be so much easier. Maybe your teen buys into the list idea, but two days later the dreaded call comes in again: He forgot! What happened to the list, you ask? I'm guessing it's on the floor under the bed, or in the dirty laundry basket. The list was never his idea in the first place, so he never took ownership for making it work.

This happened to a parent I worked with. Her daughter was a great kid, but extremely forgetful. She had a full life of sports, clubs, and friends. Every day she forgot something else. The mom was at her wit's end. The list idea went down the tubes, and Mom was desperate to find another solution. It seems that her daughter was quite artistic. Words didn't carry a lot of meaning, but color did. I suggested they get some multicolor Post-it Notes, each color representing something the girl needed to remember to bring to school. Before bed, the girl would post on the door leading to the garage the appropriate "colors" she needed to bring the next day to school. This way, as she walked out the door to go to school she would be reminded of what she needed for the day. It worked! The strategy, designed specifically for her brain, was the key.

Maybe your teen is permanently tied to his phone and would read a text from you just before he comes downstairs. Maybe it's Post-it Notes on the door or an alarm set on his phone that gets his brain focused on what he needs for the day.

There are a million strategies. Make sure the one you use is your teen's, not yours. Rather than being critical and yelling at him about his lack of organization, you can say, "I get that mornings are really hard for you. You have a lot on your mind, and it's easy to be forgetful, but we need to come up with a new strategy. I'm game for anything, and it might take a little trial and error before we find something that works, but I'm happy to help you with that. Here's what I am not willing to do anymore. I'm not willing to interrupt what I'm doing to bring you what you've forgotten. Let's just get a good system in place."

Remember, just saying "Don't forget" is not helpful. Figuring out a strategy for remembering is!

14 teen self-absorption
my teen the narcissist

Here's the Problem

At my seminars and in my coaching sessions, parents often ask, "Is it unrealistic to expect that my teen gets *me*? How about *our* hard day at work, and keeping up with the schedules and activities of our three children, and taking care of an aging parent?" How hard is it for *them* to understand that parents are also stressed to the max and can't always be available to "take me, show me, buy me"? The short answer is it's very hard. Your teen is a narcissist, plain and simple. But don't worry. It's not a lifetime personality disorder, just a short-term one.

Why It's a Problem

Your teen's brain is exploding with new connections. In fact, the number of new connections that are made in the brain during adolescence is equal to the number of new connections made during the first 18 months of life. That's a lot of brain activity to process. Just as a computer crashes when you try to keep too many applications open, so does the teenage brain. Teens are too busy trying to process, file away, or send to trash all the input from their day. Because they are seeing and feeling the world in a whole new way, they're often overwhelmed. This comes across as self-centered, disinterested, and dismissive. Your teen is in the center of his world, and right now you are a bit player, lost in the chorus. Like all good narcissists, teens see your woes only in relation to their own. So rather than be sympathetic to your long workday and commute, your teen jumps on you as soon as you walk in the door with, "Where have you been? I need you to ____." No hug. No "Hi, how was your day? You look tired. Sit down and let me rub your feet."

In a recent coaching session, a mom told me that her husband had gotten laid off from his lucrative job. They had a large, comfortable home with all the amenities that the kids had grown up with. Because of the job loss, they had to sell that home and move to a new community and rent a much smaller house. The younger kids totally got it, and like all adorable, wonderful six-, eight-, and ten-year-olds, they jumped into action. Excited about this new adventure, they started packing up their old rooms and planning for their new ones. But the 14-year-old was another story. He saw this move as a personal vendetta to ruin his life. No more beautiful game room his friends had hung out in every weekend; no more big, beautiful bedroom he had to himself. And, to boot, a move to a new school. He was up front about the fact that he was embarrassed to have kids at the new house, and he was furious with his parents for making him come to this "loser town." The easy thing would be to label this kid as spoiled rotten or entitled. It's much harder to "get" his self-centered perception of these new circumstances.

Teens are extraordinarily self-conscious. Part of this brain change is a new level of understanding and worry about what other people think about you. It's called the imaginary audience. This boy is worried that his friends (his audience) will think he's a loser now that he no longer lives in a fancy house and that his father has lost his job. For this teen—unlike his younger siblings, who see it as an adventure—the move is just one huge embarrassment.

Here's the Solution

These are stressful times for parents. Financial and job crises abound. Our parents are aging and require our help, and now that delicious love that your eight-year-old showered on you to help buffet you from the storm is absent from your 14-year-old, or at least it is sporadic. Instinctively, when kids act like brats, we tell them so, trying to teach them that selfishness is a quality you don't want to see in them. But your teens truly are capable of great love and understanding, as long as you understand them first. When you see them at their worst, it's important that, rather than criticizing, you understand. For example, in a family where parents are stretched to the limit, rather than going to the angry place of "Can't you see how hard we're working? How do you think we pay for that laptop you begged us for, or that fancy phone you demanded or the $100 jeans you're wearing? Do you think money grows on trees?" maybe you could say, "I know it's been crazy with work and taking care of Grandma. I know we haven't been around much, and maybe it feels like we haven't been able to do what you need us to do. I'm sorry. I love you and I wish things could be different, but for now we're kind of on overload." When your teen hears that you understand his perspective, his most likely response will be a grunt of "I'm fine, don't worry about it." It may not be the hug and kisses you want, but it's his way of letting you know he "gets" that you have a life too. When kids feel judged and criticized, you get the worst of their narcissism; when you understand it, you get the best of it.

15 my teen the pit bull
never takes no for an answer

Here's the Problem

Do you have a teen who won't take no for an answer? A scenario might go like this: Your teen asks you for something—a ride, money, or permission. Your answer is no. Your teen now shifts to rebuttal mode. You move to a "we'll see." Your teen sees an opening and goes in for the kill with promises and negotiations. You give an "If I see an improvement in your _____ we'll talk about it." Even though in your head it's still a no, you hope that by leaving the door open a little, your teen will stop bugging you. Perhaps this strategy worked for you in the past, but for a savvy teen, it has the opposite effect: Game on!

Why It's a Problem

Teens are extremely motivated to push as hard as they can to get what they want. Somewhere along the line, way before her teenage years, this child got an inkling that if she just kept at it, there would be a crack in the ice. Perhaps as a young child your teen was precocious and verbal, your "little lawyer." You may have unknowingly reinforced this "spirited negotiator" by being impressed by her creative use of language and persuasion. She learned early on to impress her parents with her prowess, and she believes in her power of persistence. When she was younger, these negotiations may have been about fairly innocuous requests such as TV or video game time, or the desire for a new toy or game, or wanting to stay up later. Unfortunately, the request is now for permission to go to parties/sleepovers at potentially unsupervised homes; or to purchase new-technology toys whose benefits are only additional distraction from tasks she already avoids like the plague, like homework and household responsibilities; or to attend a 9 p.m. concert at a venue 50 miles from home. Your teen's persistence in the present is predicated on what worked in the past. Enter the "pit bull."

Here's the Solution

Here are two options. First, if this is an unequivocal no, as in "No, it's not safe" or "No, it's not practical" or "No, it's unrealistic," simply state the reason, and say no. Predictably, your teen will flip out! Understand that she will not be happy with your answer. She won't reward you with a "good parenting call." Understand her anger with, "I get you're disappointed and I know you're angry with us. We can live with that." End the discussion with a shrug of your shoulders. This is your period at the end of the sentence.

Here's the really hard part: You need to be extremely consistent with this message and NOT reengage with your pit bull. Getting hooked back into the argument only energizes her. If your teen follows you around the house, or texts you multiple times within an hour after you have left the house, and continues to be a royal pain, you need to walk away. Your teen needs to see a new side of you, one that won't be deterred from a decision that you feel absolute about. This takes time and practice! You'll find this hard. Your teen will be mad at you, and that's hard. But like all things in life, this too shall pass as soon as a new request arises that you will be able to say yes to.

Here's your second option. This works for those requests where there is ambivalence on your part, but you respond with a knee-jerk reaction of no. Your teen is an expert in hearing your ambivalence and knows that this no doesn't necessarily mean no. Honesty is the best policy in this situation. Follow these steps:

> Step 1: Say to your teen, "I feel ambivalent about this. What do you think worries me about it?" Give *her* the opportunity to think this through for you.

Step 2: Say to your teen, "Yes, those things do concern/worry me. What can you do to make me feel OK about them?" Make *her* come up with a plan that may help you make a decision.

Step 3: Say to your teen, "What will the consequence be if you do not follow through?" Perhaps at this point you may be able to say yes with the plan in place, or maybe even after you have heard the plan it's still a no (then follow option 1).

Pit bulls are brilliant negotiators, but they're also young. Age and experience trumps their tenacity!

16 the teen who talks back

the kid's got attitude

Here's the Problem

Standing in front of a hundred parents, I ask them to shout out adjectives that describe their teens. *Surly, disrespectful, mean, sarcastic,* and *argumentative* top the list. Where is that fantastic eight-year-old who can't tell you enough how much he loves you and, in fact, loves you so much he wants to marry you when he grows up? So much for unrequited love!

Why It's a Problem

What's going on is really plain and simple. Your teen has now figured out that *he* is not *you*! And he will find any way he can to drive that point home to you. If you're a reader, he'll disdain books; if you hate television, he'll find the most offensive show and make sure to watch it instead of doing homework. If you're a Republican, he'll be a Democrat; if you eat meat, he'll become a vegetarian; if you're religious, he'll be an atheist. Get the picture? Teens are practicing how to stand on their own two feet, just like they did as a two-year-old, when the word "no" was a mainstay of their vocabulary. Adulthood is looming and they get somewhere in that developing brain of theirs that they will be expected to think for themselves. You, dear parents, are their guinea pigs.

Teens are self-centered, narcissistic, and demanding. It's all part of normal development. It's not just your teen; it's pretty much all teens. And to sum it all up, they just don't like it when things don't go the way they want them to go. Hello disrespect!

Here's the Solution

Having said that, this does not give your teen carte blanche to be disrespectful. I have stood behind pairs of parents and kids in checkout lines in clothing stores listening to teens talk trash to their parents. It's all I can do to stop myself from tearing those $200 jeans from that daughter's hands and telling the parent to walk away from the register. Instead I hear the parent grumble, "This is the last thing I buy for you. You don't talk to me that way, and I've had it! Now excuse me while I take out my credit card."

When your kid is mean or sarcastic and disrespectful, sticking your finger in her face and telling her she can't talk to you that way—after she just did— seems contradictory. It's an ineffectual strategy to change behavior. Sometimes parents up the ante by threatening to take away their teens' phones, computers, or social lives if they continue to talk to them in "that tone of voice." Which, of course, enrages the kid even more and requires the parent to think up more things to take away. Because after all, you can't let your kid get away with that level of disrespect.

Here are some effective strategies: First, lighten up. Humor often can be the best antidote to disrespect. Ask any bully. It's not fun to bully someone if it doesn't get him all riled up. So if it is a mild form of disrespect and he's being more sarcastic than outright mean, grab him and give him a big smooch in public and say something like, "You're so adorable when you are being a pain in the butt." This catches kids off guard, breaking the rhythm of discord. Often your kids aren't even that aware of how they are talking to you. Humor is a more powerful tool than anger.

If you move into more moderate and severe disrespect—that unmistakable, whiny, yelling, demanding thing—try to refrain from yelling, "Don't talk to me that way! You're grounded!" Instead, you might say, "I know you're frustrated. I know you think I'm being unfair [fill in the blank with whatever you're being accused of]. I get it, and I would like to hear what you have to say, but not when you're screaming at me." And now you walk away, without getting hooked back into a screaming match.

If you are a last-word kind of person, this will be especially hard for you. But understand that your teen has stopped listening to you anyway. He's put his metaphorical fingers in his ears by yelling as loudly and as long as you. Take a deep breath and go away! Sometime later, perhaps you go into his room and say, "I would like to hear what you have to say." The key here is to just listen. Don't get defensive and don't feel like you have to keep making your point. If, after you've listened, you haven't heard anything new, feel free to say, "Thank you for saying this in a way I can really hear. I get that this is important to you, but it just can't happen, and I am sorry about that." Give a little shoulder shrug, and WALK AWAY! Your teen is not going to thank you for saying no. He'll be frustrated and angry, but if you disengage you're helping him to prevent that anger from becoming even more disrespectful toward you. If you stay, nothing good will come of it.

Using the example of the mom in the store, when your kid starts to abuse you when you are actually doing something nice for her, there is only one thing to do: Without yelling or saying how ungrateful she is, JUST STOP DOING IT. If you're in the car taking her someplace she wants to go—a friend's, the mall, CVS—and she starts in with you, rather than launching into the "I've had it. Why should I ever do anything for you when you treat me this way!" rant, say nothing. Turn the car around and go home. If you are in a store, drop the $200 pair of jeans on the counter and vamoose. You are teaching your teen about the reciprocity of relationships. If you ground her or take her phone away because she treated you badly, there's often no lasting effect because there's no relationship connection. But when you stop yourself from doing the things you usually love doing for your teen, there is a powerful connection. So the next time your teen has been disrespectful and comes back 10 minutes later for a ride to the mall, you can say, "You know honey, I love doing things for you, but you just screamed 'I hate you,' and now I need some time to get over it." No need for sarcasm. Actions always speak louder than words.

17 the messy room
to clean or not to clean

Here's the Problem

I think that the number one complaint I hear from parents of teens is, "My kid is such a slob!" Opening the door to your teen's room is like going down a black hole. Dirty laundry mixed with the clean, new (expensive) clothes stomped on, turned inside out, and looking unappreciated for the sacrifice you made in purchasing them. You wonder how hard it could be to hang up clothes, put away laundry, bring the dirty glasses and plates into the kitchen, and generally live like the civilized human being you thought you had been raising. No matter what you suggest, no matter what you threaten, it falls on deaf ears. You make deals, you cajole, you yell, and nothing seems to work. Every time you walk by that closed door, knowing what's inside, you get that pit in your stomach, and the veins in your neck stick out just a little more. You feel helpless. You wonder how it all came to this. What happened to those days of yore when all you had to do with your kid was ask (or threaten with no TV) and the deed was done?

Why It's a Problem

Your kid could care less about her room. Her new developing brain is consumed with thoughts way more interesting, nerve-racking, anxiety-producing, and exhilarating than the clothes on the floor. The idea may pop into her head, "Oh, I'm supposed to clean my room," but it's fleeting.

Here's the Solution

First, take an honest look at the room. I visited a family recently where the room issue had become all-consuming. When the dad opened the door to show me his son's room for an objective assessment, I was expecting the worst, but what I saw was a room that kind of looked like mine at home. Yes, there were some clothes on chairs and tables, and some shoes flung around; the comforter was askew on the bed, but honestly, it wasn't that bad, and it made me feel a little guilty about my own lack of neatness. (I ran home and cleaned my room.) It's all about expectations. Are you a neat freak who expects everyone to have the same standards you have for yourself? You may be setting yourself up for a fall. If, however, the room is over the top in crazy-making chaos, here are a few suggestions.

You can start a conversation with "I get it, I know you're fine with the way your room is [try not to judge and be critical here] and you and I have different standards, but it does make me crazy. Can we figure something out so that we can both be OK? Maybe Sunday nights we do it together so at least the week can start out fresh." If your teen rejects that approach, try this: "I get that keeping your room more organized is not that important to you, but it does make me crazy, so I just want to let you know that I will be coming in once a week to make sure that the ants, bedbugs, and other disgusting creatures will be set free by ridding your room of trash, dirty laundry, and food stuff." This may be motivating for teens if they don't want their parents entering their bedrooms unsupervised!

Another approach: The next time your teen asks you for a favor like a ride or money for a new outfit, you can say (with no sarcasm), "You know honey, I would love to help you out. Just let me know when you have cleaned up your room and I'm there for you."

Parents, here's the thing about room cleaning: If it really bothers you, do it yourself! This also makes you look good in your kids' eyes since you won't be yelling at them about it. You can now focus on other things to yell about. But the bigger payoff is that it gives you access to your kid's room. Your kid's room holds a lot of clues to his mental health. It's not really just about being messy, but do you get a sense of depression, anxiety, and chaos? That's way more important than the underwear on the floor. There can be unforeseen benefits too. I once worked with a parent who made the leap to clean her son's room, and lying on the floor, out in full view, was a poem he had written about his family. In this poem was a declaration and recognition of the love he had for his parents. In fact the poem was titled "I Am from Love, I Am from Life." She sat down and cried. This mom and son had been at war for weeks over his room, his attitude, his everything, and here she found this nugget of gold that gave her new perspective on their relationship.

Find a way to make the messy room work for you. Try to get him to take responsibility, but if you see that his busy schedule (up at six, school till three, practice till six, shower, dinner, homework, Facebook, texting, bed at eleven) truly doesn't allow much free time, especially to clean his room, then the gift of "I get it, you have a crazy schedule, you have a lot on your plate, I'll take care of this piece for you" at least makes this power struggle go away. You are not giving in or giving up, but giving to!

PART TWO
Just tell me what to do about...
Keeping My Teen Motivated and Engaged in School

18 why can't my teen do better?
how to assess achievement

Here's the Problem

A dad is worried about his son, who is a junior in high school. He's worried about his son's lack of self-direction. How will his son ever be able to think about the college application process and all that it entails? His son can't even get himself out of bed in the morning! He's unable to work independently to get any of his homework completed, especially any kind of research or writing assignments.

Why It's a Problem

I wanted to know what role he and his wife play with regard to their son; what kind of strategies did they employ to keep him motivated and on task? The plot thickened. It seems that the dad is heavily invested in his son's future, like most parents. Dad has a strong relationship with his college alma mater and would be heartbroken if his son didn't continue to carry the torch for his beloved college. His older daughter is currently a student there. In pursuit of this goal, the father has become CEO of his son's life.

For example: His son plays varsity football. He's a good player, but not phenomenal. Dad attends all his games armed with a video camera, as many parents do, so that 20 years hence they can show their grandkids how cute their dad was in a football uniform. Not this dad. He videos each game so that he and his son can engage in a play-by-play of all his moves, to evaluate what he did, right or wrong. Imagine how this teen feels when he has had a bad game? Not only does he have to answer to his teammates and his coach, but he also has to go home and face "the man."

Another example: This teen has ADHD and is on medication to help with concentration and attention. When this teen has a paper to do, or an assignment with some heft to it, the father is all over him, requesting draft after draft, editing and re-editing his son's assignment. Both are often up till the wee hours of the morning when the paper is due. Needless to say this teen becomes overwrought and overwhelmed by his dad's expectations of him. The mom reports that the son is so afraid of his dad's disappointment in him that he has yet to speak up for himself and tell his father to back off! Which would be my therapeutic intervention. No wonder this kid has a hard time getting up in the morning. Facing another day of trying to measure up must be exhausting for him. No wonder it takes him so long to complete an assignment; it never feels good enough.

Many parents have a "grand plan" for their kids. How wonderful it would be if everything went according to plan. But your kids bring their own strengths and weaknesses, passions and personalities, to the table. And they don't always match with what you see for their future. This dad's alma mater couldn't be a worse match for his son. Maybe he is good enough in football to get in, but academically he would be lost at sea, feeling inadequate and never quite good enough. A professional football career is clearly not in the cards, but a failing academic experience could injure him more profoundly in the long term than a full-out tackle.

Mom is right. This teen is so overmanaged that he is developing few skills in becoming an independently motivated and self-directed person. He doesn't need to because his dad is doing it for him!

Here's the Solution

Please do not set your teen up for failure. Be realistic about who your child is. Help *him* to set realistic goals for himself and allow him to become the person he is meant to be. Adolescence is all about identity development. *Who am I? How am I the same as or different from my parents, my friends, or my favorite character on* Gossip Girl? "Identity Foreclosure" is a term we in the healing arts use to describe relationships like the boy and his dad described above. The dad has foreclosed on his son's ability to develop his own sense of who he is and who he wants to become. The son is so busy becoming what dad wants that he may be losing his "real" self in the process.

It's easy to focus on outcome instead of process. Perhaps you have a teen whose grades, from your perspective, are subpar and you're frustrated by her lack of effort. (See Chapter 20 for specific strategies with homework.) Objectivity is the most powerful tool a parent can use. Take a step back and evaluate the kinds of expectations you have for your teen. Are they realistic? Are they more about what you want for your teen or what the teen wants? Are you expecting all A's from a teen who is involved in positive, engaging after-school activities and has an active social life? These too are important elements for a well-rounded, happy, successful adult life. B's are good too! Grades, number of tackles in a game, or lead roles in the school play are not predictors of success in life.

19 studying and learning vs. texting and facebook

strategies for time management

Here's the Problem

Getting teenagers to do homework has always been a struggle. Nothing new there. But the distraction quotient has multiplied faster than bunnies in a hutch. First it was computers, then cellphones, then texting and tweeting and Skyping and Facebook, and now smartphones that can provide entertainment and distraction 24/7. Who knows what new communication tool is about to launch. But you can be sure that whatever it is, your teen will want to have it.

As a college professor, I see a direct correlation between these new technologies and the attention my students give me in class, as well as their ability to do their work outside of class. I yearn for the good ol' days when my students had only my face to look upon, instead of their laptop logged into Facebook and their fingers too busy texting and tweeting to hold their pens and take notes.

Here's where you come in. Do not feed your teen's addiction. If you are planning to send your teen off to college, this is the time, right here, right now, to help develop self-discipline. You'll be spending enormous amounts of money to educate your kids, and if they don't have an awareness of their use of technology and how it affects their attention and learning, you'll be wasting your money.

Why It's a Problem

The research is unequivocal. A recent study at Stanford found that though teens can manipulate multiple devices simultaneously, their brains are competing for the most important and interesting stimulation. The most stimulating wins out every time. Facebook versus calculus: Which do you think wins? I'm guessing that over the past few years, parents of my students have not been happy with the D's and F's I've had to give their kids. As more and more teens are given smartphones and laptops at earlier and earlier ages, their concentration quotient decreases. By the time they get to college, if something is deemed "boring," they can find instant entertainment elsewhere.

I know this is a problem because more and more of the coaching requests I receive are from parents frustrated by this and who feel helpless to intervene. When report cards are sent home, I get an avalanche of calls, especially from parents of high school juniors who see college options slipping away as their kids' grades dip.

Teens are obsessed with their friends; always have been, always will be. And now that they have a plethora of means to stay in touch, they do just that. Teens are impulsive, spontaneous, and full of new thoughts, new feelings, and new possibilities. Every new text or Facebook post reflects a new opportunity. "Ooh, I think this boy really likes me. He said to text him a sexy picture of myself!" Really, how can a request like that compete with studying for a quiz in government?

Your teens need help developing discipline. It doesn't come naturally, and can be extremely painful, especially for those kids who previously have been given unlimited access without supervision. They will not be happy. But that's life . . . really, that's life. And that's perhaps one of the most important lessons you can teach your teen. As the Rolling Stones sang, "You can't always get what you want."

Here's the Solution

Helping your teen to develop self-control won't be easy. But if you can wait 10 years for a "thank you" from your child when he or she is a young adult who finally gets how important it was to have been shown the light, it will be a thank-you worth waiting for. You wouldn't let your kids eat junk food 24 hours a day, or watch TV for hours on end, or any number of other things that, as an adult, you know are detrimental to development. No, you stand up to those kids and do what you have to do. For some reason parents are terrified of doing this with texting and tweeting and Facebook. JUST SAY NO. Here are some strategies:

Selfcontrol.com (a Mac application that can block access to Facebook for up to 24 hours), FamilySafeMedia.com for PCs, Freedom (which disables all Internet access on Macs for up to three hours), and Leechblock (which blocks Internet for Firefox browsers) are three applications that can be downloaded onto your teen's computer from the Internet.

Each of them automatically disables Facebook or other social networking sites at scheduled times. The reason that these are so effective is that it takes the power struggle out of the equation. Being the Facebook police is no fun, and teens are amazingly crafty. This enables you to sit down together and say, "I get how much fun Facebook and Twitter are for you. I know that you're worried that if you're not always checking in then you might miss something. But it's important for you to have some time during the evening when you're not checking. This is not only so you can concentrate better on the work you have to do, but also for the future. Just like I wouldn't let you eat candy till you throw up, I can't let you become addicted to something that in the long run will be harmful to you. I know you don't see it now, but once you're on your own, you need to have some experience and practice at just focusing on one thing, whether it's college or a job. I want you to be successful in life, and if you're angry with me forever, so be it, I'll deal. Let's discuss together the times you are willing to be shut off."

This strategy should be enforced for cellphones as well. All carriers will shut off and turn on the phone according to your needs except for smartphones. This is why I hate smartphones for teenagers. You literally have no control unless you take it away. So take it away, at least during homework time! There should be cellphone-free hours, and absolutely no cellphone use in bed.

If you have fifth through eighth graders, this will be easier. Your kids are still babies. But regardless of your kids' ages, *you* are in charge. When your young teen gets a cellphone there should be rules in place, such as "You can use your cellphone until 6 p.m.; then I get it. I will return it to you at 8:30 so you can check back in with your friends until 9:30, when the phone will be shut off." This is not just about homework; this is your chance to limit from the very beginning your teens' dependence on their cellphones. It's good that your teens want to connect with friends, but not for hours on end.

If they give you a hard time, you can always say, "I get that this sounds hard, but you have a choice. Either you cooperate with this plan and choose to have your phone, or you choose to fight me, and I choose to take the phone away." You're in control.

For older teens, especially if you have noticed a drop in grades due to a lack of concentration, use incentives for changing behavior. Most teens are desperate to get a driver's license, and they need you to sign off on it. POWER! Many of your teens want to go to college, and they need your help to get there. POWER! You can say, "We've noticed a steady decline in your effort and your grades. Part of that is related to your need to stay connected to your friends at all times. In order for us to feel confident in your ability to drive and concentrate on your driving, and for us to feel confident in your ability to handle the freedom of college life, we need to come up with a plan that shows us that you're capable of 'shutting down.' We're willing to help you get your license and allow you use of the car when we see that you can be without Facebook and texting for some part of every night. The same thing goes for college and all the work it takes to go through that process. We're willing to do everything we can to support and help you with it all— visiting schools, helping with applications, and money—but only if we feel you're showing us your ability to focus on what you need to do to get there. Let's set some goals for this next term. What grades are you willing to work for, and what are you willing to do about limiting Facebook and texting and all your other apps during a few hours in the evening? This is important stuff, honey, because if you have a hard time saying no to yourself and focusing on homework, even for a short time, that does not bode well for driving or college. We do not want to set you up for disappointment or failure."

If you've already given your teen some kind of smartphone or iPad or iTouch, take it away. Say you made a mistake and realize that allowing unlimited access to the Internet 24 hours a day is a setup for temptation. Most adults can't deal with it either. This is just not the right time to add any more distraction to your teen's life.

Check your cellphone logs and make sure your teens are not texting during school. For many kids it is yet another distraction they can't resist. Even if they're not using it during class, they are thinking during class what they will text when they get out of class. Shut their phones off during school time.

If you have bought your teens their own laptops, make them do their homework in the kitchen. I also recommend shutting off your wireless modem before you go to bed. If all else fails, take away their laptops. If they make the argument that they need the computer for school, then take them to your public library and let them work on the computers there.

This is not easy. Unfortunately, many parents have to backtrack, not anticipating the allure of these devices and the addiction factor. If you want your teen to develop good habits and focus, you have to take the lead on this. The temptation factor is just too strong, and it's unrealistic to expect that your teens will be able to shut down and shut off on their own. The research about this stuff is abundantly clear: We're doing our teens a disservice by not setting better limits. Yes, your teen will be mad; yes, your teen will say you are the worst parent ever; yes, your teen will say, "I can't wait to move out of this friggin' house." But you know better. The bottom line is, your kids love you regardless, maybe just not at this minute. Wait 10 years.

20 the plight of the homework avoider
it's not just laziness

Here's the Problem

I was at the gym the other day talking to a group of parents while waiting for our spin class to begin. I asked them, "What hot-button issue are you having with your teens?" With resounding unanimity and gusto, they said, "HOMEWORK." Some things never change. Homework avoidance has been an issue between parents and kids since homework was invented. Truly, doing something that isn't fun isn't fun!

Back when those teens were in elementary school, they loved doing homework. Homework *was* fun. It makes a kid feel a little grown up. It was usually project-oriented and gave them a chance to tap into some creativity. Most important, it pleased their parents when they did it. Elementary school kids are developmentally wired to want to please their parents. But teenagers? Not so much.

Why It's a Problem

Here is what's behind homework avoidance:

→ It's usually boring; no more building dioramas.

→ It's often hard. Schoolwork gets more challenging in middle and high school, and it's a rude awakening not to feel smart all the time.

Especially if you have a teen that breezed through elementary or middle school having to do almost no homework. Getting good grades was easy breezy!

→ It's cumulative. Perhaps a few assignments have been missed, and now they are in the deep, dark hole of being behind, feeling like they'll never be able to catch up. Better to just avoid altogether.

→ Fear of failure. Many teens worry that their work is just not good enough. Perhaps they are perfectionists. If they don't do it at all, then they won't be exposed for being "dumb" or not as smart as people think or expect them to be.

→ They're tired. Days get really long with after-school activities, jobs, and sports. Homework requires a level of concentration that can feel daunting and exhausting.

→ And most important, drum roll please, they want to "hang" with their friends, even if it's a virtual hang.

This is a lot for parents to battle against. Most of it isn't what you actually see when you walk into your teen's room. These are the invisible issues. What you do see is multiple screens on the computer, the phone in your teen's lap, fingers tapping away in conversation, a downloaded TV show or movie playing on their iPhone or iTouch, and yes, there may be a textbook open somewhere in there. The underlying feelings of frustration, anxiety, and boredom are cloaked by the copious amounts of avoidance behaviors.

Here's the Solution

First of all, close your eyes and visualize yourself at this age. How many of you eagerly sat down to do homework? I have visceral memories myself, dragging the phone with its long cord (I'm old) into my room and whispering away for what must have been hours to my seven best friends. Keep in your mind your own experience of "homework" before you criticize your teens for their lack of attention to what you know is the most important thing they should be doing.

Your tendency may be to storm into your teen's room and in a disgusted voice yell, "Get off that damn phone and shut down Facebook or I am taking both away! Either you do your homework and get your priorities straight or [fill in the blank here with your threat du jour]." But you can go another way and say, "I get how boring some of this stuff is" or "I know this math [or this French or this chemistry or biology] is really tough, and I know you have a lot going on in your life these days. It must be hard to focus on your homework." Or (this is especially for the kids who may have ADD or ADHD) "I know how hard it is for you to have to sit and concentrate on all this stuff at one time." Let them know that you get that this is hard, frustrating, boring etc., AND that there is nothing wrong with them for feeling this way. When teens feel understood, it frees them up to listen and become an active participant in the process. Then you can get to the planning piece. You can say, "Let's figure this out so we don't have to argue about it every night. We can't change that you have homework and that we expect you to do it, but we can figure out a way that works for you." If you're worried that this homework thing is a chronic problem, make sure you communicate regularly with the teacher. Emailing at the end of the week to find out about missing homework gives you a leg up on the "I did it" avoidance technique for many kids.

If your teen is a procrastinator and has dug a "homework hole," you might consider hiring a "homework buddy." These can be high school students for your middle schoolers or college students for your high schoolers. They are not tutors. These older "mentors" can be helpful in structuring your teen's homework time and motivating her to do the work. Why? Because they aren't your teen's parents!

I suggest that they pick your teen up after school or early evening and take him to the public library, where there are usually study rooms. Try to schedule them to come at least two or three times a week for hour-and-a-half sessions. Their job primarily is to sit with the teen during homework and be available for help if it's needed. Having a homework buddy helps your teen to develop homework routines and rituals, important strategies for homework success. It reframes homework from a lonely, isolating, boring experience to something your teen will look forward to. Having a homework buddy who doesn't judge or express disappointment can free teens up to figure out what gets in their own way in completing assignments. A visit to Starbucks for a mochaccino after homework doesn't hurt either!

Maybe your teen can't sit for two hours at a time. Work out a plan where he works in the kitchen for 30 minutes, without phone and computer, and then takes a 15-minute break to chat with friends. Many phone carriers and Internet companies have parental control programs where you can program phones and computers like DVRs, scheduling when they are on or off. This is a great tool because you and your teen can come up with a schedule together, and it takes away all the arguing to turn off the phone or get off Facebook. The bottom line is you want to avoid the power struggle of "Do your homework!" versus "You can't make me!"

Which, by the way, is actually true. If teens think that parents are trying to MAKE them do something, they will do everything in their power to show their parents just how powerless they are by just not doing it. Understanding them and planning with them teaches them to look at what gets in their way to do what they need to do and to figure out strategies that can support them. This is a life skill they'll need to take with them in the next phase of their lives. If parents take control of how and when teens do or don't do their homework, the teens will never learn how to manage all the distractions of life that are coming their way.

21 the drama of exams
a strategy for success

Here's the Problem

Finally, something parents and teens can agree on: Midterms and final exams stink! For many teens, the few days before these exams will be a time for cramming. I remember when I was in high school. On the weekend before exam week, I would sit on my bed and read chapter after chapter in some boring U.S. history textbook, attempt to memorize random French vocabulary, buy and read every available Cliff Notes on the books I was supposed to have read for English, memorize the element table in chemistry, and then basically throw the towel in on geometry theorems, knowing that was just a lost cause. I get anxious just writing all that down! It makes me supremely grateful to be a grown-up and free from memorizing anything.

For parents, the dread of final exams comes from knowing what this weekend will be like for you. You are gearing up to play multiple roles: motivational speaker, prison guard, therapist, and tutor. You go from saying, "You can do it, you're a bright kid" to "Shut off that damn phone, get off Facebook! How do you expect to get anything accomplished?" to "Honey, I know you're anxious, exams can be scary" to "Let's go over this together; I'll quiz you." Your teen both needs you and hates you. Be prepared for a Dr. Jekyll and Mr. Hyde experience.

Why It's a Problem

Just as I am overwhelmed thinking back to those years, your teen is over-whelmed thinking of all that has to be studied. Of course, as adults we know if he or she had only kept up with the work all along, this exam thing would just be a matter of reviewing material, not learning it for the first time. But we know that because we've had 30 or 40 years to reflect on it!

Teens feel anxious about expectations they have for themselves and about their parents' expectations of them. They're also anxious about how they'll measure up against their peers. Remember, after the exam their friends will ask, "What did *you* get?" That's a lot of worry!

Here's the Solution

Lecturing on what they *should* have done has no place here. Start from where they are. Your teen will need some help in finding the forest through the trees. Everything he has to study begins to look like one huge amount of material, a mountain too big to climb, a personal Mount Everest. Help him to come up with a structure and time frame for each subject, working in breaks for food, Facebook, and texting time. I implore you: Bribe him to turn his phone over to you. The research on teens and multitasking is conclusive. Though they can manage physically to text, Facebook, and read simultane-ously, their brain can't. I recommend alternating 45-minute work segments and 15-minute breaks.

To get this process started, you can say, "I get that this will be a tough weekend for you. I know how overwhelming it must feel to prepare for all these different subjects, so let's come up with a kind of schedule to break it down so it won't feel so overwhelming."

The research on effective study skills shows that it's better to study a sub-ject for a shorter period of time, let it sit, and then come back to it. The schedule of study should reflect this. A little bit of this, a little bit of that. And repeat.

For those of you who have teens with test anxiety, here is a strategy. A study done at the University of Chicago reports that when students write for 10 minutes prior to an exam about their thoughts, feelings, and worries about the test, it prevents test anxiety during the actual test taking. The hypothesis is that test anxiety can lead to poorer grades and lower test scores. The findings are pretty powerful. Kids who were prone to test anxiety improved nearly one full grade if they were given 10 minutes before an exam to write down their feelings. The researchers believe that worrying competes for computing power in the brain's working memory. Simply put, if the brain is working on the worrying, then it can't also work on retrieving information needed for the test. The writing exercise empties the brain so it can give its full power to the test. Sounds good to me!

You're in survival mode. You're the helicopter that brings in life-saving food and water. Keep it positive, and keep it calm. The bottom line: There isn't that much you can do. You can lead your teen to water, but you can't make him drink!

22 the report card
a call to action

Here's the Problem

It's report card time. Parents open the envelope with trepidation and anticipation. Some glance quickly, scanning for standout grades in either direction.
Others take their time, one grade at a time, and one comment at a time. Until
that comment, the one that makes veins pop and hearts pound. "Johnny is a
good student, but he's missing three homework assignments and because of
that his grade is a C instead of a B."

Such a message may be new to you. Perhaps in previous years your teen
led a quieter, less social life than other kids. Studying hard and striving for
good grades was her mission. But what is this? Where are the A's and B+'s
you've grown accustomed to seeing? For other parents who were hoping for
a fresh beginning and a new semester full of promise, there's disappointment
that it's the same old same old.

Why It's a Problem

Though your first impulse may be to barge into your kid's room or to start
in on this the moment she walks through the door, I encourage you to pause
for a deep, cleansing breath. You're probably feeling duped by your teen. You
asked her over and over and over again, "Did you finish your homework?"

and the answer was always, "Yes." You probably asked over and over, "Did you make up those missing homework assignments?" "Yes!" But here is the living proof and the evidence of that lie. You are storming.

Here's the Solution

Your teen expects the storm. She is primed and ready with excuses, explanations, and promises for change. Consider this an opportunity to approach this in a new way. You may feel like starting the conversation with, "This is what happens when you spend too much time on your phone and with your video games. In this house, schoolwork comes first!" Instead try this: "Hey honey, let's go over your report card together." Let her read it out loud. After each grade and comment say, "So what do you think about what your teacher said and how she graded you?" I know this is hard, but you really have to just listen and let your teen do the talking! You may hear some complaining, some "It's not my fault the teacher is mean." You may hear some denial: "I didn't know that was missing." Then ask, "What do you think got in your way? Was the homework hard? Was the homework boring? Is it hard to settle down and do homework when you get home? Too many distractions?" You want to help your teen analyze what to do differently. If you yell and criticize and dictate what needs to be done differently, you won't engage *her* in the process, and nothing will change. The goal is to use this report card not as an indictment of bad study habits, but as a roadmap for moving forward. If you don't put your teen on the defensive and focus more on your wanting her to feel successful, you will find her more willing to have a conversation with you and figure out a plan of action.

Incentives are a good technique for motivating change. Incentives are successful when they are based on short-term goals. Promising a new car if she gets all A's and B's for the whole year is a goal that's too far in the future. Initially it's exciting, but when a teen is slogged down in boredom in December, June and the car are part of a future that's too distant to care much about. Teens are present-centered beings. Better to do weekly incentives. Work with teachers to get regular reports on assignment completion. Don't wait for progress reports to get the bad news. Request them weekly if this has been a major issue. Weekly incentives for positive reports from teachers can be money, manicures, iTunes downloads, clothes, anything that motivates your teen. Who doesn't like a little reward for hard work? Ask any adult who gets a bonus!

This is not about the grades! This is about your teen mastering material and developing a curiosity for learning. This also goes for your teen who comes home with a straight A report card. If you focus on the A's rather than on "I'm so proud of all your hard work and how much you learned this term," you'll have a teen who's motivated to learn because of the external motivator of making you happy, rather than the power of the learning itself.

The most important message is not to label teens as lazy or unmotivated. This does not change behavior. Providing motivation, structure, and understanding does.

23 summer reading

thank you teachers, for ruining my last few weeks of summer

Here's the Problem

As the end of summer closes in, crumpled-up summer reading lists are being found and resurrected by parents everywhere. Most kids have spent the summer avoiding parental queries about the reading by saying, "I'll do it. I have the whole summer, just leave me alone!" Well, the whole summer is now down to three weeks and the books were long ago purchased, Kindled, or Nooked. "If I buy you a Kindle/Nook, will you do the reading?" Your teen, panting like a dog that sees a new treat coming its way, has promised that yes, yes, yes, he'll do the reading if you buy him off—I mean buy him a Kindle/Nook.

Why It's a Problem

If your teen isn't a "reading for fun" kind of person, then summer reading is just school without the classroom. It doesn't matter what form the book is in; it's still reading, and it's definitely less exciting than, say, sitting on the couch texting, Facebooking, videogaming, watching a movie, or studying one's own navel.

Summer mode means deadlines and homework are out of sight, out of mind. It's not the reading itself that your teens don't want to do. It's more that doing the summer reading reminds them that going back to school is just around the corner. And that's a corner they absolutely do not want to go around!

Here's the Solution

Here are a few strategies to get the reading done before school starts and before you have to resort to the threats of no phone, no computer, no life until they finish their reading. Sit with your teen and add up the pages that need to be read by the start of school. Get out the old calculator and divide that number by the number of days left before school. Now you have a PPD, or pages per day your teen needs to read.

When you break it down this way, it's far less intimidating. Many teens have three or four books to read, and all they see are hours and hours of reading ahead of them. Pretending it doesn't exist is much easier. Having to read 20 pages a day may not seem as bad.

Set aside a reading time. Not on *your* schedule, but a time of day that feels right to your teen. Get *your* book, take your teen to Starbucks, buy her an iced cappuccino, and read together for 30 minutes or an hour. Pair the reading with something pleasurable.

Another suggestion is to get the books on CD. Some kids may be more motivated if they're hearing them rather than reading them. Put them on in the car when you're driving together or on the family's summer road trip. Make it a family affair! Or give them one of those "old-fashioned CD players" and let them listen with earphones; bring it to the beach and they can tan and "read" at the same time.

If your teen continues to be resistant to follow-through, pair reading with favors. For example, if the PPD hasn't been completed and your teen asks for a ride, money, clean laundry, etc., you can say, "I would love to help you out, but I noticed you haven't done your PPD today, and I don't really feel like complying with your request until you do. I get that this reading stuff is hard for you, but it's just something you have to do."

Get creative. Nagging teens to read will not get the job done. You have to "understand" their resistance, not just criticize it. Help them to develop a plan that makes the impossible seem possible.

24

senioritis-parentitis

surviving the application process and tips for successful college visits

Here's the Problem

If you have a senior in high school, I'm sure your teen is suffering from a condition that is commonly known as Senioritis. As a parent, you're suffering from a corresponding and complementary affliction, Parentitis.

Symptoms of Senioritis include intense procrastination, increased surliness (if that's possible), increased avoidance of parents and home, and rejection of all suggestions on how to complete college applications.

Symptoms of Parentitis include high anxiety and sleepless nights, weakened eyesight from too many hours looking at college websites on the computer, and fatigued fingers from keeping up with college application submission deadlines on the family calendar.

For parents, the anticipation of their child all grown up and ready to go off to college is both exciting and terrifying. Remembering their own college years, they can't wait for their kids to experience all the wonderful things they did, which may have included finding and marrying the love of their life, making lifelong friends, finding a passion and/or career, and making memories that last a lifetime. But there is trepidation as well. What if my teen doesn't get the grades and SATs that will get her into the college *I* want, I mean *she* wants, to go to? What if he doesn't write his essays on time, or worse, what if they're bad? What if she doesn't get her applications in early or at least on time? What if we don't have enough money to send them to the school of *our*, I mean *his*, dreams? What if my best friend's kid has better grades and better SATs and gets his essays and applications in before mine, and he gets into the school I want my daughter to get in? And what if _____?

This is the stuff ulcers are made of.

So you become the college Nazis. "You will get your essays done this weekend, or you won't go out!!!! You will go with us to visit colleges on the weekends we want to go! You will go to SAT tutoring or you will be grounded!" And for all this commitment and time and money you give to your teen in support of this college journey, what do you get in return? "Leave me alone. I'll do it!"

Why It's a Problem

The whole college admission process is a lesson in letting go. You can nag, you can hound, but the bottom line is you can't "make" your teen get this work done. To combat Senioritis, parents must pay less attention to the symptoms and more attention to the underlying issues. If you label the procrastination as laziness and avoidance, your teen gets defensive and angry, feels criticized, and ends up procrastinating even more. Not exactly the outcome you were hoping for.

Here are some of those underlying issues:

1. Your teen feels completely overwhelmed by the additional responsibilities of the college process, over and above the normal load of school, activities, and friends. Choosing which schools to apply to, completing the applications and essays, and finding teachers who know and like them enough to give them recommendations gets added to the "to do" list. This is in addition to improving or maintaining good grades (because God knows everyone keeps telling teens how important those first-semester senior grades are). And by the way, could you get the lead in the school play? Score a few touchdowns? Do a great community service project? And—only if you have time—would you mind curing cancer? It will look great on your college application.

Not only are they feeling their own sense of impending doom about where they will end up, but they also feel your expectations, their school's expectations, their friends' expectations, not to mention their grandparents, aunts, uncles, neighbors, and friends of their parents asking every time they see them, "So how's your college application thing going?" Imagine what it feels like to have everyone who has ever known you be so interested in the rest of your life. This is expressed through anger and avoidance.

2. Because your senior is acutely aware of all that you want for her, and she obviously has her own fantasies and expectations, she's full of anxiety and dread for that day when the acceptances or rejections show up online or in the mail. *What if I don't get in anywhere, or I don't get in where I want to go or where my parents want me to go?* Ultimately this whole college process feels like the biggest report card of her life, like an evaluation of who she is as a person. You get an A when you get in where you want to go, and a big, fat F when you get rejected. The worry teens feel about disappointing their parents and disappointing themselves is palpable. Often it comes across as anger and avoidance.

3. Though your senior is excited for this next step, change is not easy. Leaving you guys is terrifying, even if they're not showing it. But believe me, the more angry they act toward you, the more scared they are feeling inside. This is a useful defense mechanism. They're also terrified of leaving their friends, their lifeblood, their support, and their source of acceptance. This fear, too, comes across as anger and avoidance.

You get the picture. The anger, the procrastination, and the avoidance are all expressions of feeling overwhelmed and anxious. Your teen is engaging in magical thinking. "If I put this off long enough, I don't have to deal with the consequences." This is all *completely normal*. This is the first and single most important decision they've had to make in their lives. They have no previous experience on which to draw that tells them that it will all turn out OK. As parents, you know it will. But they really aren't willing to take your word on that.

Here's the Solution

Avoid starting every conversation with: "Did you start your essay? Did you do your common app? Did you talk to your teachers about a recommendation? You know you're running out of time!" Try this instead: "I get how overwhelming this all feels. You have a lot on your plate with school, and sports and college stuff; I know I would just want to get in bed and cover my head for the next six months. How can I help? I'm happy to do whatever you need. Think of me as your administrative assistant, not your boss. I don't want to have to harp on you all the time. I know how annoying that is. Can we come up with a plan together? Maybe the plan includes me bugging you. Let's break this up into smaller projects, so it won't feel so overwhelming. If I do start to annoy you, let me know and I'll back off. I love you, and I want you to have the kinds of choices you deserve. We don't want to spend this year arguing with you constantly; we want you to take ownership. This will be a sign to us that you're ready for college. If you choose not to participate in this process, then that will be a sign to us that you might not want or aren't ready for the independence of college. What do you think? Are you up for this? Or are you feeling you might want to take a year off after high school to get yourself ready? Whatever you choose is fine with us, but commit to one or the other."

Now develop an action plan. Sit at the computer together with your teen doing the typing. Print out the plan, including dates he hopes to have things completed by. Put it up in his room, on the refrigerator, and in the bathroom if you need to. Put those iPhones, iTouches, and iPads to good use with electronic reminders for the weekly goals he's made for himself. Be creative. Just saying, "Get it done!" is not helpful. Working with your teen to come up with a plan is.

But please, and I'm begging you here, do not do it for them. Do not come up with *your* schedule or *your* way of doing things. This is a setup for disaster, because they will not take ownership of *your* plan. When you see them screwing up "your plan" the arguing commences. And, by the way, it is no problem if you want to use some incentives like money, upgraded phones, clothes, trips to the Caribbean (only kidding on that one). But seriously, whatever works. Businesses thrive on using incentives. If it's OK in your job, why not in theirs?

Now, a few college visit tips. Remember this is your teen's opportunity to just soak in the atmosphere. This is not the visit where she's worried about what the biology labs look like, or course selection. I know that's what you're interested in. But for these first visits, you really need to zip it up and let it be about your kid. She's looking at the students and wondering, *Are there kids here I could imagine being my friends? Does the campus feel like a place I feel comfortable and safe in? Could I sleep in this dorm and imagine myself feeling at home?* This is what interests your teen. So walk along beside her, keep a low profile, and if you have questions ask them another time. There will always be the second visit if they like the school and, most important, if they get in! Many kids avoid college visits prior to acceptance because they worry that if they "fall in love" with a school and don't get in, it would feel devastating. So keep that in mind.

On the drive home from a college visit, try to refrain from sharing *your* impressions the second you get in the car. Often parents are much more enthusiastic about a school than their teen is, and that shuts him down from talking to you. Give him time to digest the visit. Some teens will start talking right away; others need time to process. Remember that visiting colleges makes everything about the college process real and scary. They may need some time just to sit with it all. So if they immediately put their earbuds in, just let them be. On your way home, stop for a bite to eat, some ice cream, or coffee, and maybe ask, "So what did you think?" in a calm, neutral voice, and see where it goes.

This will be a challenging year, but a year full of growth for all of you. Be patient with the process, continue to "get" their struggle, and provide support and understanding. This too shall pass, and soon enough you'll have the car packed and ready for this next step, the arguments about applications and recommendations already forgotten. The bottom line is it will all get done, one way or another, and if it doesn't, take that as a sign that your senior is telling you that this might not be the year for college. Senior year is a rite of passage for everyone. Just hold on tight and enjoy the ride.

eenie, meenie, miney mo, to which college should I go?

a roadmap for decision making

Here's the Problem

It's that time of year when high school seniors, after receiving either a "thick or thin" envelope, have all the information they need to make this difficult decision: *Here's who accepted me. Now where do I go?* How easy this decision would be if there were only just one criterion: *Which one do I like best?* Unfortunately, due to today's financial climate, other more pressing questions must be answered: *Which college is the least expensive? How far is it from home and what are the transportation costs? And most important, what's the financial aid package?*

Prospective college students may still be stuck on question one. They're looking through the prism of an image they've created for themselves of living in the dorm, lolling about on the campus, and perhaps joining a fraternity or sorority whose house they saw during the college tour. They may have a favorite and are stubbornly sticking to the fantasy of attending that college and that college only. Much to your chagrin, this is the college that's the most expensive, has given no financial aid, and is the farthest away, making traveling home for spontaneous weekends impossible. Your heart is breaking. On the one hand, you want so much to be able to give your child what he wants. You've bought into the fantasy, and perhaps over the year you've participated in discussions that gave your teen the message that you supported this choice. But now reality has met fantasy.

In addition, your teen probably hasn't given much thought to what it *really* means to go to a small school versus a big school, a city school versus a rural school, a school where being in a sorority or fraternity is the only gateway to all that's social, a really cold climate versus a warm one, etc. I have worked with many parents whose teens had miserable first semesters at their "favorite" colleges and came back home to work until they could transfer to a school that was a better fit. Sometimes this can be avoided if you help your teen to ask the right kinds of questions *before* making this big decision.

Why It's a Problem

Teens are ruled by emotionality, not practicality; by fantasy, not reality. Most high school seniors are clueless about the financial costs of college, unless it's been clear from the very beginning of the college search that they would have some financial responsibility. For many kids, college is seen as an entitlement. It's just something you do. They don't give much thought to the dollars and "sense" of it. Many parents feel uncomfortable sharing their financial information with their children and choose not to talk about the money aspect. But when those envelopes appear in the mailbox, the reality of what the next four years are going to cost hits.

The fighting begins. You assume your senior will understand the hard facts and be grateful to you for paying for college at all. Though disappointed that he can't go to his favorite school, he'll understand that this is reality and he'll know he will be happy somewhere else. Ah, if it were just that easy. But they won't understand. In this moment, they're not thinking about you and your financial pressure, or the two sisters coming up behind him that have college in their future and will also need your financial support. Teens don't get the sacrifices most families have to make for their kids to go to college. They are selfishly thinking only of themselves. They are self-centered because teens are naturally that way and also because of the myriad of emotions they're feeling now that college is a reality. These feelings can interfere with rational decision making, especially after a "thick" envelope arrives in the mail.

Here's the Solution

First, understand with them how stressful this time is. "I get that you have so many things on your mind. It's going to be hard to leave your friends and start over. Even though we annoy you, I know you'll miss being home, and starting somewhere new is both exciting and scary. We get all that, and we know that this all plays into your decision about where you want to go to school. In order to make this decision together we have to get past the emotional weight, which is how much you love the school, and look at the reality of it."

The first order of business is discussing the financial piece. This can begin the elimination process. If distance is an issue, have your senior go online and find the price of travel back and forth to this school. Have her look at how many times she anticipates making this trip and put that dollar amount on the list. In addition, add in tuition, room and board costs, spending money costs, etc. Go through this same procedure for all accepted schools, including any financial aid that's been awarded. Look at these final amounts together and put down the dollar amount you feel you can contribute. Where there's a shortfall at a school, perhaps at her "favorite" school, ask your senior how she proposes to make up the difference. This is an important discussion and process to go through with your teen. Rather than just saying something is too expensive, or too impractical, make her an active participant in the nuts-and-bolts calculations.

When you have a list of financially affordable schools, go through each with a fine-tooth comb. Play devil's advocate and offer real-life scenarios that—given a particular college's size, location, population, cost, etc.—could impact your teen's life should she choose that school. The college ordeal is almost over, and this last piece of investigation may be your most important. You're teaching your teen to take ownership over this very important decision. It's probably the biggest decision your teen will ever make. How it is made will impact the next four years of your teen's life.

26

what to expect from your high school graduating senior

letting go

Here's the Problem

What can you expect from your graduating teen the summer before his freshman year? NOTHING! No really, I mean nothing! Here *you* are, feeling all warm and fuzzy after graduation last weekend. Nostalgic for your little girl or boy all grown up and ready to go off on a new adventure. You pull out all the old photo albums and gaze longingly at the years that have whizzed by, and you try to prepare yourself for life's next stage: having a child move away from home. You find yourself welling up with tears as you do your teen's laundry and when you pick up the dirty dishes he's left on the floor of the family room, knowing that in just a few months his bedroom will no longer have that whiff of dirty laundry as you walk by. Everything annoying and maddening your graduate did before graduation suddenly seems sweet and memorable, at least for a few days.

Of course you expect your high school graduate to be equally wistful. But instead you're blown away by her seemingly instant sense of entitlement. Where are the thanks for the wonderful party you threw for her? Where are the thank-you notes for the generous gifts given by friends, family, neighbors, and anyone else who has ever known her? Suddenly, your graduate is nowhere to be found. You're left in the dust, with "Bye, won't be home for dinner, may be sleeping out, don't know when I'll be home!"

Why It's a Problem

You're dumbfounded. After all, this last summer at home should be filled with family dinners, cozy family movie nights, a family vacation, and shopping trips to Bed Bath & Beyond. If only they would stay home long enough to make some plans.

Well, you can kiss those plans good-bye. All their nostalgic moments are being saved up for their friends. The friends they'll be leaving in only a few short months, maybe never to be heard from again, or at least until Thanksgiving. Prepare yourself. Your graduate will be glued to her friends this summer. They will take top priority over everyone and everything. And if you don't understand the importance of "the last summer before college," your feelings will be hurt over and over again. My advice: Don't take it personally. The process of saying good-bye to high school friends takes a good two months. Of course they'll miss you too. But you never really go away, and truly, many of their friends will. How many of you still have close relationships with high school friends, that is, before Facebook brought everyone right back to you?

Your teen is also hiding away a lot of anxiety and worry. Worry that he won't be happy; worry that he'll be homesick (yes, they really do worry about that even if they aren't saying it); worry about keeping up with all the schoolwork without you around to keep him on task; worry that he won't know how to deal with money issues, laundry issues, and all the other millions of things for which he's been depending on you. And you know how your graduate will deal with all this worry? By being a big pain in the butt! By sounding irritated with you, bothered by you, and ready to fight with you. Don't bite! Rather than looking and feeling like a needy little child, your teen will behave "as if" you are not needed at all. It's so much easier to leave when you think your parents are annoying you than when you feel overwhelmed by love and sickness at the thought of living without them.

Here's the Solution

Your teen's absence this summer will feel like a betrayal. Don't let it become a source of anger between you. You might have this conversation: "I get that saying good-bye to your friends is hard. I know how much you'll miss them, and you're probably worried that you won't find anyone as wonderful as [fill in the blank with some real names]. I get that you want to spend as much time as you can with them this summer, and I want you to do just that. But honey, your old Ma/Pa are gonna miss you too. I hope that we can find some time together as well before you go. Let's figure out how best to do that."

Your graduating teens may also now feel that rules no longer apply to them. After all, they're 18 and all grown up. In some ways, they're right. In only a few short months they really will be on their own. So instead of having a bunch of rules they will flout all summer, take it day by day. Let them know that you "get" that they want to be independent this summer, but you still need to know that they are safe. Set up a system (not rules) so that they can keep you posted and in the loop so that you won't need to be checking up on them. Rules may be resented, but a system seems less controlling. Your teens are teaching you to let go. Let them!

27

what to expect from your college students when they return home

Here's the Problem

There's a feeling of excitement for both college students and parents as they anticipate the "coming home" experience. For parents it's magically matured college students anxious to spend quality time sitting around the dinner table discussing world events, joining them in the family room for popcorn-filled movie nights, sleeping in bedrooms where beds are made every morning and laundry is put away, and engaging in polite banter that keeps parents in the loop of their plans and whereabouts. Ah, it sounds too good to be true. And it is! Sorry to burst your bubble, but your kids are still your kids, and there has been no magical transformation.

For your returning college students, home is a place where home-cooked meals appear instantaneously and where clean laundry is available upon request. They imagine a place where the family car is at their disposal day or night and questions about where, when, and with whom they're going are completely absent from their parents' lips now that they're college students. Well, they're in for a rude awakening as well.

Why It's a Problem

It's all about realistic expectations. The chaos of returning college students may be comforting at first. Your kids are excited to be home, back in the bosom of the family, all cozy and warm. But they're still kids, and they've come from a place where freedom isn't "just another word," but a way of life. This can be a huge adjustment for parents of homebound college students. Yours will chafe at that first glimmer of "So where are you going, and what time will you be home?" or "Just because you have been away in college, when you're home there are rules, and we expect you to follow them." Ooh, let the games begin.

Here's the Solution

It's time for a new game plan. I am not suggesting a free-for-all, letting the cards fall where they may, but a recognition that life has changed, your kids have changed, and you can never go back. You might say, "We're so excited to have you home, and we get that being away from home and then coming back is going to be an adjustment for all of us. I get you've been on your own. It's probably felt amazing to be in control over your own life. We get that you'll be out late and that you want to do what you want to do, but here is what's going on with us. We have gotten used to having our car to ourselves, not worrying about your whereabouts and your safety, and not being responsible for laundry, cleanup, and dirty dishes left wherever. We want this visit to be good for all of us, so let's try to come up with a workable plan."

If you can anticipate with your now older and somewhat more mature teen all the annoying stuff that will happen, you'll be ahead of the game. It's important to understand that this isn't about enforcing "rules" but looking for a partnership with this emerging adult. Recognize that the old rules have been outgrown and that new "agreements" based on mutual respect need to be forged. The revolving door is now in place as your kids come back and forth from real life and the joys of freedom to the welcoming and sometimes smothering arms of their family. There will be times when someone gets caught in the door. It could be you, and for sure it will be your kids. But the door will keep moving because it has to. It's the law of nature.

28 # the bully pulpit
strategies to ward off a bully

Here's the Problem

The media is full of stories about the trauma of bullying. Those of you who have watched your child cope with bullying have experienced this trauma firsthand. Research on bullying suggests that a child's brain actually changes as a result of this emotional trauma and that it has lasting effects well into adulthood. Clearly this debunks the myth that kids will be kids.

Though many communities have put into place antibullying measures and severe consequences for kids who bully, most kids are ill-prepared for real-time situations. In the moment when a kid is being mercilessly teased and taunted, throwing out a "this isn't allowed" isn't going to be helpful to that victim.

Being a bystander while you watch your "best friend" bully someone can be almost as painful as being the victim. Like victims, they too are at a loss for words, knowing that the "right" thing would be to step in and stop it. But because of the hyper-self-consciousness of adolescence and their own feelings of anxiety, discomfort, and vulnerability, they choose to avoid a response that could make them feel even more uncomfortable: "If I step in, the bully won't think I'm cool" or "If I step in, the bully will turn on me." It's a crime of helplessness.

Why It's a Problem

Bullying is all about power. It's only fun to bully someone as long as the victim stays in a down position. Self-consciousness, shyness, passivity, and awkwardness are no weapons when it comes to savvy, confident teens who love the power of making someone feel less than. Maybe puberty has been unkind to your teen, and weight gain, lack of height, and acne have turned your once carefree child into a teen who hides under big sweatshirts, hats, hair, bowed head, and silence. Perhaps he has been made fun of during gym class for running too slow, or in the cafeteria for eating too much during lunch, or who knows what, and he has absolutely no idea what to say or do when it happens. Unfortunately, saying nothing is worse than saying something, at least to a bully. It's an opening for more! Sadly, teens that are bullied are often so humiliated by their own lack of action that they never share this blight with adults who could support or help. And so the cycle continues.

Like many new experiences in life, having someone deliberately want to humiliate them is a possibility that most teens are not prepared for. As adults we hope that this type of situation won't happen to our kids, or that our kids won't be the perpetrators of bullying. So until there's a crisis, there's usually no discussion.

Here's the Solution

Giving teens strategies for those moments in life when they are unprepared is paramount, especially if you see some change in your teen from happy and carefree to notably quiet and isolated. Look objectively at your teen. Can you see that the changes of puberty have not been kind? Don't wait for him to come to you. He probably won't. It's much too embarrassing to tell your mom and dad that kids are picking on you. Victims of bullying want to be able to handle it, not run to Mom and Dad "like a little baby."

Maybe someday while you're walking the dog or taking a ride in the car together, you might say, "You know honey, I've noticed you don't seem as happy as you used to be. I've noticed you don't hang out with X and Y any-more. Have they moved on to some new friends? Have other kids been giving you a hard time? I know that can happen. You know, if that's happening, I can help you with that. We can come up with things to say back to those kids that will make you feel strong. I am always here to help." And then just leave it there. Don't ask a thousand questions. You have opened the door; you've shown that you're aware of a change, and that you're there for support.

It may be that your teen has not had to deal personally with bullying, but I'm sure she is aware of it going on around her. You might say, "A friend of mine just told me that her son has been having trouble with bullying at school. I was so shocked to hear that. I'm guessing that must go on at your school too. Do you know anyone who has had to deal with this? I hope if you ever have any experiences with bullying, that you feel you can come to us for help. I promise we won't call the school unless you give us permission, but I know we could help."

When your teen does open up, here are some strategies you can share: Humor and sarcasm are effective tools to help counter the bully's attempts at humiliation. For example, if you have a teen who is overweight and has been teased about it, help him to come up with some quick retorts—to be delivered with strength and power—like: "Big is beautiful, thanks for the compliment," "Ya think?" or "Ooh you're so observant" or "I'm looking for a trainer, want to help me get in shape?" Let your teen know that responding to a bully with silence or avoidance inflates a bully's confidence; showing self-confidence deflates it.

To help your teen who might be faced with being a bystander, you can say, "You know honey, I get there might be a time when you see one of your friends bully another student. I know it's hard to take a stand sometimes even though you know it's the right thing to do. Kids can be pretty cruel, and I know I would be afraid that kid would turn on me. So here are some things that might help. Maybe talk to your other friends and together make a pact that when this bully starts in on someone, you'll all help. That way no one person feels like they have to take this on alone. There's power in numbers. The bully is counting on the fact that they have the most power. But if you and your friends band together, you're the ones with the control. You can say things like 'You're an idiot, we're out of here,' or 'Hey man, take it down a notch.'" Give them a script and an action plan. In those moments of real stress, it's hard to do the right thing.

Helping teens feel strong and competent to handle what comes their way is important. It's realistic to anticipate that at some point yours may be a bystander to bullying or a target for jealous girls, insecure boys, control freaks, and people who bully for the sheer joy of it.

loyalty in teens can be harmful to their health

penn state, a case study

Here's the Problem

For a time, the sexual abuse scandal on the campus of Penn State was a media megastory. It was bad enough that a longtime assistant football coach was caught in the act of raping a young boy of nine in the football locker room showers, but adding insult to injury was the cloak of silence that protected the coach and the Penn State football program from investigation. Avoiding scandal was more important than protecting the young boy and other victims. This raises the important issue of loyalty versus accountability, responsibility, and safety. When does the duty of being loyal to those closest to you no longer apply?

Teens often find themselves in situations when this very dilemma is questioned. There is nothing, and I mean nothing, that stands in the way of a teen and his friends. If you ever criticize even the most obvious fault of one of his buddies, the gauntlet is thrown down. The cardinal rule "never talk bad about my boy/girl" has been broken, and you will pay dearly for breaking it. Secrecy and avoidance will become your teen's go-to response whenever you try to bring up this friend in conversation. This lack of objectivity about their friends can often put teens in situations that are scary and unsafe. They become caught in the bind of doing what they know is right versus protecting their relationship at all costs.

Why It's a Problem

Perhaps your teen has a close friend that is depressed or perhaps even suicidal, is engaging in self-destructive behavior, has a serious eating disorder, or is abusing drugs and/or alcohol. Maybe your teen has been with a friend who's been drinking or doing drugs, and though *she* won't get in the car with him, she won't grab the keys away from this compromised driver, leaving the possibility of a drunk-driving accident in the hands of her drunk friend. Loyalty, secrecy, and trust are powerful promises. The *risk* of losing this friend, should she break this oath of loyalty, is usually stronger than the possibility of actually losing the friend.

Here's the Solution

Though not a precise parallel, the Penn State case can be used as a valuable tool to help teens talk about loyalty versus safety. You might have this conversation: "Hey honey, have you heard about this story at Penn State? [If not, share it.] Pretty scary stuff, isn't it? I'm guessing there must be times that you're in a position of questioning whether you should do something you know is right, but worry that it might get a friend in trouble. Maybe you have a friend who's depressed, or drinks, or does too many drugs, or is involved with illegal activities, or is in a scary relationship and talks to you about it but makes you promise not to tell anybody. That's a lot of responsibility to carry around. Imagine how you would feel if your friend ended up getting hurt in some way, when you could have gotten them help, but because you were worried about breaking their trust, you didn't. I'm always here to help you with this stuff. If you were worried that I'd call the parents or the school, I would never do that without your permission. I'm here to help you deal with it all. I would never want you to think that loyalty trumps safety. Making sure that your friend is safe is way more important than whatever secret they have given you to hold."

This is an important issue to address with your teen. There is too much at stake not to.

the agony of a ninth-grade boy
what it feels like to be the youngest boy in the school

Here's the Problem
If you are the parents of a ninth-grade boy, you may be seeing an epidemic of weekend lethargy, which includes social isolation, empty friend syndrome, and video game overdose.

Why It's a Problem
Here's my diagnosis. Being a ninth-grade boy is the lowest of the low in high school land. The loss of social status is huge. While ninth-grade girls enjoy being the youngest, newest, and appealing to older boys, ninth-grade males have become obsolete in the social hierarchy that is high school. They are often the shortest, not having experienced the eagerly awaited puberty-fueled growth spurt. It can sometimes feel like they're living in the land of the giants. Their acne may be in full bloom, further eroding their confidence in the daily pageant of "who's cute," a favorite pastime for teenage girls. Furthermore, they've left a middle school where they were top dogs. Perhaps they were the best athletes at their middle school, or they had the lead in their school musical, or were president of the student council. Now here they are in high school, a place they've dreamed about for years, and SLAM, reality hits.

Maybe your son makes one of the school's athletic teams, but being the youngest, he gets little playing time and ends up spending most of his time on the bench. Or if he's lucky enough to be a good athlete, he gets to play and the upperclassmen are resentful because this young punk gets more play than they do. These older guys feel free to show their resentment. It's a no-win situation.

Adding insult to injury, he may be losing his best buddies. Ninth grade is a year of so many changes and transitions, including friends. Some kids are more ready and more interested and have enough confidence to jump into the water, no matter how cold it is. They are ready to party, find girls, and hang with the big guys, leaving their old friends in their wake.

Here's the Solution

The bad news is that this year will feel like the longest year for you. You're at the same time feeling heartbroken for your son, seeing him mope about aimlessly, at odds with himself. Frustrated, you wonder, "What the hell is wrong with him? He should get off that damn couch and do something!"

So here it is in a nutshell: They don't know what to do! The rules have changed and they don't have the playbook. So when your son walks in from school every day and gives you a sneer and a grunt, asking him what's wrong will probably garner a scream of "NOTHING!" Don't be offended; just get that a million things are wrong, things that got stuffed down all day at school, things he may not even be consciously aware of: a stare from an older student, a fumble on the field, an embarrassing wrong answer in math, and the list goes on. When the weekend comes, cozying up in the safe haven of his room is as much as he can muster. Saying things like, "Why don't you call a friend?" or "Why don't you invite someone over?" only reinforces for him that he's a loser. Maybe that "friend" he would have called is now off with a bunch of new friends, partying in the park, which is something he's neither ready for nor interested in, thank God.

The good news is, this too shall pass. This is a moment in time, and as he gains confidence, height, and clear skin he will begin to join the human race again. He'll find new things he feels excited about, and new people to hang with. For the time being, because it won't last long, just enjoy his company. My prescription: Make a big bowl of popcorn, settle into the couch, and watch a movie!

31

teens who feel left out

"why don't they ever call me?"

Here's the Problem

A parent asks, "How much should I intervene in the social life of my 13-year-old daughter?" Mom reports that seventh grade has been a good year. Her daughter is an A-B student, plays multiple sports, and seems to be liked by her peers. Mom's worry is that though she seems engaged with her friends when she's at structured activities like her games or school plays, when the weekends come, she's "home alone." She sees the other kids getting together on the weekend, but she's not an "initiator" and instead waits around for friends to text her. When they don't, she feels like a loser. Mom questions how much she should help her with this. She's worried that she might become one of those helicopter parents.

Why It's a Problem

During the middle school years, you absolutely can't find a more self-centered bunch of kids. This girl's friends aren't calling or texting her on the weekends because they're too busy thinking about themselves and their own plans to think about whether anyone's been left out. There's new excitement at this age as they explore the idea of a "social life" versus a "playdate." To see this in action, just walk through your town center on a day when middle school lets out early. These young teens are practically jumping out of their skins as they roam through town in huge numbers, ecstatic with these new-found feelings of independence and grown-up-ness. They're focused on how they look, how they act, and who they're with, period. They love their friends, but mostly because they see their friends as a reflection of themselves. When the weekends come, only the strong survive.

Those teens who are obsessed with the powerful new feelings of independence will be extremely motivated to make something happen. On Friday night or Saturday afternoon, texts begin to fly around town asking, "What are you doing?" "I don't know, what are you doing?" If you don't get into the texting "game" you're left out of it. This, I suspect, is what's happening with the seventh-grade girl. She needs to get into the action. No more sitting on the bench and waiting for the coach to put her in. In these early years of adolescence, friendships don't run deep. This girl's friends aren't thinking, "Oh, I wonder what X is doing today. Let's give her a call." If your teen doesn't send a text to someone saying, "Hey, what's up for today?" she'll end up "home alone."

Here's the Solution

If you have a son or daughter who is waiting to "get asked to the dance," here are some ways you might help. Understand that this middle school transitional time can leave your teen a bit overwhelmed and confused about the change in how to "do" friendships. Many teens at this age are clueless about this new social life. If you can't invite a friend over to play with Barbies or Legos any-more, then what else are you supposed to do? You might say, "I have some errands to do near the mall on Saturday. I would be happy to drop you and some friends off at the movies, the batting cage, or McDonald's. Why don't you text X and Y and see if they want to come?" Even if that plan doesn't work, it will get your teen into whatever other action plan is in the works as she gets into the texting conversation with her friends. Most likely what she'll get is "Oh, so-and-so and I are going to X, wanna come?" And that will be that. Middle school is a transition time. Many kids are used to parents orchestrating their playdates, and now they're a bit adrift in the sea of plan making. They've no experience doing it, and it may actually go against their basic nature. This is especially true with boys. How many husbands do you know who get on the phone and make the plans for weekends and vacations? I rest my case!

the bad seed friend

what to do about the friend you wish your teen didn't have

Here's the Problem

A mom wrote me the other day with this dilemma: She has a 14-year-old daughter whose friendship with a girl a year older had caused her daughter a great deal of trauma last year. They succeeded in helping her separate from this girl. There had been a big team effort from the school and the daughter's therapist and a lot of love and caring from this mom and dad. Parents, school, and therapist saw a huge change in this 14-year-old. She began to have a happier disposition, reconnected with old friends, and had a lot less anxiety and misery—a win-win.

Mom thought this friendship was a done deal. This new school year has been a good one, with little drama now that this friend is out of the picture, not only emotionally, but physically as well, having moved on to an alternative high school for teens with attitude and behavioral issues. Everybody breathed a sigh of relief. And then, there was a request from her daughter last weekend to go to a semiformal dance a few towns away with a friend Mom loves . . . and the girl from last year who had caused her daughter so much angst! Mom was shocked. She thought this girl was gone and forgotten. But here she was again! Mom had been keeping up with this girl—and her drug- and alcohol-fueled partying escapades—by reading her daughter's Facebook.

There was a simple answer to this request from her daughter: NO. Mom understood her daughter's disappointment, but her decision was firm. Her daughter did not understand and was furious. She pulled out the "you're the worst parents ever" line, which is a surefire guilt producer. The parents wondered whether they were the worst parents ever. Mom wrote, "She seems to gravitate to these kids because they 'accept' her. She doesn't have a huge group of friends, and she's trying to make new ones but is having trouble. These troubled kids all accept her, because misery loves company. Help!"

Why It's a Problem

This is hard work for a teen. There's nothing more flattering than to have someone show interest in you, especially the "bad girl." These girls or boys are usually charismatic, fun, risk-taking, and manipulative. They often prey on more passive, insecure types. They can seem especially attractive to those kids because they do all the "friendship work" for them. They make the plans and orchestrate their social life. It can feel quite seductive for this unconfident teen to have someone in her life who makes her feel so important.

When you see your teen with someone you feel could pull her into situations you think are unsafe and/or emotionally unhealthy and who potentially could have a detrimental effect on her future, your mama/papa bear claws come out. You share your "insights" with your teen, expecting her to listen, learn, respect your opinion, do the right thing, and get rid of this bum! But because your teen is now biologically and emotionally driven to think just the opposite of you, in a show of "well I'm not you," she's suddenly more motivated than ever to dig her own claws into the bad influence as a show of independence.

A major task of adolescence is "separation." This means developing the ability to stand on one's own two feet in preparation for life as an adult. There are some things your teen is willing to admit that you know more about, albeit reluctantly, such as academic issues. But friends are completely off limits to you. This is an area of your teen's life she feels is her birthright. *Be damned with what my parents think!*

Here's the Solution

The bottom line is you can't control your teens' friendships. When your teen hangs out with kids you don't like, who you feel bring nothing positive to the table, you may feel helpless in your ability to intervene. But, and this is an important *but*, you can have *influence*, which is different than control. In the example I mentioned, the parents, school personnel, and the therapist definitely had influence in helping this 14-year-old see that this friend was a downer, and the *daughter* was able to separate from her.

Certainly, saying no to situations that you know will be unsafe is a number one priority. These parents knew that allowing their daughter to go to a dance with a girl who is a known "partier" was unsafe. Maybe you'll get the "worst mom/dad" award that weekend. So be it. The bigger job is to continue to help your teen navigate this relationship and help her to be successful in forming new ones. You can say to your teen: "I get how X can be a fun friend. Tell me what you like about her." And second, "So what do you think worries me about X?" Lecturing your teen about all the ills of this "bad seed" will only make her want to defend this kid. You want your teen to articulate what's attractive about this kid and to articulate what she thinks worries you about that. This makes your teen an active participant in the discussion and plants seeds for her own work in processing the yin and yang of this friendship. Most important is to listen without judgment. When we lecture and talk at teens, most likely they'll shut down. When we show respect for their opinion, they open up.

Helping kids—especially those kids who lack confidence—find positive relationships is the bigger task. Sometimes it takes a little sleuthing. If you know your teen has an interest in something but is shy about getting involved, you can go behind the scenes. For example, perhaps your teen is a technology wizard. You could go to the guidance counselor or technology teacher and ask if he or she might personally approach your teen to join the computer club, where they are designing video games. Teachers often have no idea that a student has a hidden talent unless someone like you tells them. This gives your teen access to a whole new group of potential friends. Perhaps your teen isn't into sports or theater or anything at school. Help him find a job, internship, or community service project where he might have the opportunity to meet other teens. If your teen has a hard time in the friendship department, you need to help him gain access to a wider network. Maybe that's a job or volunteer work or a school activity. But what you need to know is that this kind of teen will not be the one to go find these opportunities. Saying things like, "Why don't you sign up for [fill in the blank]" will fall on deaf ears. Whether it's finding new friends or signing up for activities, they just don't have the confidence. The work is helping them develop that confidence.

Your teen may not fit this profile. He may be confident and engaged with a friend or groups of friends you just don't like. Perhaps they are the wilder group, or the more alternative clique that you worry might engage in unsafe and scary behaviors. The advice is the same. You can't say, "I don't want you to hang out with those kids. You're not allowed!" Unless you plan on home-schooling your teen, they *will* be seeing those kids every day at school, eating lunch together, and hanging out. Telling your teen, "You're not allowed" when you truly have no power to say that makes you look ineffectual. Better the devil you know than the one you don't. Invite these teens to your house and get to know them. You'll have much more influence with your teen when you're making judgments about his friends if they're based on actual experience. Control what you can. Use supervision and withholding permission for activities that are unsafe.

Navigating and understanding friendship is the work of adolescence. Part of that process is going to the buffet of friends and trying out some new "dishes." Ultimately this work influences who we let into our lives and how we do it.

getting to know your teen's drinking personality

33

what motivates your teen to drink or do drugs?

Here's the Problem

Adolescence is a time of life that's full of experimentation. Teens are literally seeing the world and all its options through a new brain. The beer in the refrigerator, the vodka in the liquor cabinet, or those funny little cigarettes some of their friends may be smoking are suddenly of great interest. In childhood, they were puzzled about why grown-ups drank something that tasted so "yucky." Now they understand that it's less about the taste and more about the way it makes you feel. For a teen who lives in a brain built for wild and crazy emotional moments, drugs and alcohol are a perfect gateway for those experiences.

In order for parents to help their teen navigate through the minefield of drugs and alcohol and stay safe, they need to understand their teen's personality and what drives this behavior. This process is not a "one size fits all." If parents don't understand the unique and underlying motivation for their teen's experimentation, then advice and consequences will be ineffective. Who's *your* teen?

Why It's a Problem

The Risk Taker. When these teens were three-year-olds, they ran instead of walked. These kids showed no fear. A big slide, a climb to the highest rung of the monkey bars, straight downhill on a pair of skis, roller coasters, scary movies, you name it, they're always game. This is what makes being around them so much fun and, of course, terrifying. Your parent mantra: BE CAREFUL!!!

These teens' brains have turned into a risk-taking machine, and the drive for dangerous fun is a powerful motivator. Now it's not steep slides, but fast cars, power drinking, and being up for trying and doing just about anything. Obviously this puts them in a vulnerable position.

The Shy and Anxious Teen. These teens were very cautious children. They had difficulty in new and unfamiliar situations. They stuck to their parents like glue, feeling uncomfortable around people. They probably spent much of their time at home with their siblings rather than out on playdates, and they needed encouragement to make friends. Over the years you might have seen these children grow more comfortable through involvement in sports or other activities that gave them a sense of purpose. But now as teens, the expectations to be social, chatty, and charming can be overwhelming. These teens are usually well liked. They are easy to be around and make loyal friends, especially when they're with the kids they feel the most comfortable with. But now there are new expectations. Romantic feelings, flirting, and acting cool don't come naturally to shy and anxious teens, who are even more self-conscious than their peers. This makes these teens very susceptible to drugs and alcohol. Pot mellows them out, and alcohol gives them a false sense of confidence in the situations where they feel the most awkward and vulnerable.

The Fun-Loving Teen. Who doesn't love this kid, the one everybody wants to be around: fun, easy to talk to, easy to get along with, and able to rally a crowd into action. High in emotional intelligence, this teen is a natural leader who loves a good time. These are wonderful qualities that will help this teen to be extremely successful as an adult. As a teen, this kid will ALWAYS be up for a party!

The Impulsive Teen. As a child, this person needed to be reminded a thousand times to "look both ways before you cross!" This teen interrupts, shouts out in class rather than raising his hand, and has little patience for waiting around for anything. This teen will not want to take the time to think much through. This rashness, in addition to the impulsivity that all teens have, can be a double whammy and a potentially lethal combination.

The Teen in Crisis. Perhaps there is a divorce or separation that is weighing on your teen. Maybe there's been a recent death in the family, an ill grandparent, financial problems, or a parent's job loss. There may have been a recent breakup with a beau, or a feeling that she has disappointed you yet again with low grades. There could be a million things that your teen is good at masking, making you think she's handling it. But this can be a particularly at-risk time for teens. They feel bad, and booze or drugs make them feel better.

Here's the Solution

The first step is acknowledging and accepting who your teen is. Temperament and personality are not things you can change. Giving teens the gift of acceptance for who they are, and loving them because of that, opens the door to communication, self-reflection, and understanding. Here, by category of teen, are the keys to help your teen stay safe:

Risk Taker. You can't tame this beast, but you can talk with it. A conversation might go like this: "Honey, you know what I love about you? I love that you're always up for a new challenge. You're game for anything. In life, that can be a wonderful and exciting quality. Unfortunately right now as a teen, that 'up for anything' could put you in a lot of unsafe situations. You really need to understand this about yourself so that you can put the brakes on before whatever you are 'going for' gets out of control. I do worry about how you'll manage drinking and driving and drugs. I know there are times when you and your friends challenge each other and get caught up in one-upmanship. When this involves drugs or alcohol, fun can turn into danger really fast. Let's come up with some ways that can keep you safe."

Anytime your teen leaves to hang out with friends, go through this process. Depending on what the plan is, brainstorm potential unsafe situations that might come up. Get your teen to exercise that frontal cortex, the thinking center of the brain, with strategies for safety. At the least some seeds have been planted.

Shy and Anxious. You might have a conversation like this before your teen heads out to a party or hang with friends: "Honey, I know that sometimes when you're with friends in a group situation you feel uncomfortable. You might feel that drinking will make you more comfortable. This worries me. You might feel that to fit in and be relaxed you'll have to drink or smoke pot. That can be a dangerous precedent to set in your life. It's more important for you to learn some strategies to make yourself comfortable in these situations rather than relying on alcohol or drugs to do that for you. I have confidence that you can figure out how to be in groups and be comfortable. Here are some strategies: Don't show up alone somewhere. Try to make plans to go with a friend. Walking into a group with someone else means you have someone to talk to from the beginning. Offer yourself up as the designated driver. This gives you an important role to keep your friends safe, and they will really appreciate that. There are lots of things we can come up with. Let's work together on this."

Fun-Loving. Here is a conversation for your "life of the party": "You know what I love about you, honey? Everybody always wants to be around you, including me. You're a fun person. I only worry about that now because you're always up for a good time, and I know that sometimes that can mean alcohol and drugs. We're going to need to come up with some strategies to keep you safe, when your party-hearty head takes over." The strategy for risk taker works well here as well. Another strategy is to make sure he has a designated party buddy who reminds him if they're drinking too much or too fast, and makes sure they don't do something unsafe. Another may be that due to a past history of heavy partying, you'll always be picking him up after a party, even if you have an older teen with a driver's license. Most teens will not overindulge when they know a parent will be the chauffeur service.

Impulsive. Criticizing impulsive teens over and over again for not thinking things through will not be productive. But educating them about their nature may be. It can be comforting for them to know that you understand how hard this can be. "You know honey, I totally get how hard it is for you to put the brakes on something when you want to go full force ahead. Your mind and your body just say 'GO!' This worries me. Your natural tendency is not to think through before acting because you get caught up in the moment. Maybe we can start a count-to-10 rule. When someone says, 'Hey, let's do . . .' rather than just going for it, you take a second, take a deep breath, and literally count to 10 before you act. This may truly save your life one day!"

Teen in Crisis. Your job is to help label the feelings you imagine your teen may be experiencing. Make observations. Don't ask questions. "You know honey, I notice you're spending more time in your room since the divorce and that you avoid hanging with me. You seem to be sleeping a lot. I really get that this is a tough time. I know sometimes when people go through tough times they might find some comfort from drinking or smoking pot. I worry that when you're out with your friends this might become a way for you to cope with what you're feeling. I get that can be an easy way to feel better, but ultimately you have to deal with what's making you feel bad. You know you can always talk to me, but that might be hard for you right now, so I am going to set you up with some counseling to get you through this crisis."

Understanding, anticipating, and problem solving are life skills that will keep your teens safe now and are tools that will be helpful to them for the rest of their lives.

34 keeping your teens safe if or when they choose to drink
a successful strategy

Here's the Problem

No parent is prepared for the first time his or her teen is caught drinking. You have lectured till you were blue in the face about how dangerous drinking is. One parent, the child of an alcoholic herself—with a brother who's an addict—had conversation after conversation with her teen about the dangers of addiction and the possibility of genetic addiction for him should he become a drinker or drug user. She thought that she had done a brilliant job of putting the fear of God into her 15-year-old! Like many parents, she was naive and hadn't yet "teen-proofed" her home. This process involves locking up any and all temptations, including beer and wine as well as all the prescription drugs. Where else do you think teens get their booze? One evening she came home unexpectedly and found her 15-year-old with a beer. "It felt like a PTSD reaction after all I had gone through with my family," she recalls. Many parents have had or will have the same reaction, an OMG moment: "Is this the beginning of my child's downward spiral into alcohol abuse?"

Why It's a Problem

Okay, this is a deep-breath moment. I don't care how much and for how long you have been warning your teens about the ills of alcohol and drugs. This

DOES NOT temper their curiosity. It may delay it, which honestly I think was the case for this 15-year-old. Most kids are presented with plenty of opportunity well before they're 15 to drink or try drugs. Some succumb to the temptation either at a house party, hanging in the park with their friends, or at a sleepover. Most teens have been dreaming of this "first." Adolescence is a time of many "firsts." First experiences with romance and sex, first experiences with parties free from parental supervision, and definitely the big "firsts," alcohol and drugs. Their new teenage brain has alerted them to all the possibilities of life. They want to know what the big deal is with this alcohol and drug stuff. They've heard all kinds of stories: bad ones from their parents and "awesome" ones from older siblings, other kids, and the media. Frankly, it would be more shocking to me if a teen weren't curious.

Here's the Solution

How you react to this first experience will be the foundation for whatever else happens with your teen regarding drugs and alcohol. So you want to take your time and not just react with anger, disappointment, and punishment. If you go to that place, then your teen will go further underground, avoiding you and lying, something you want to avoid at all costs. Here's what you can do when that "first time" happens.

In a loving, calm tone, say, "Honey, first of all I'm sorry we left the booze in the house. I think it was a temptation we didn't give enough thought to. Having it so available, along with your curiosity and desire to try it, is a bad combination. I am sorry we put you in that position." This helps to start a conversation from a supportive place rather than an angry place. Your teen will be more likely to actually talk with you. If you caught your son or daughter boozed up, but not on alcohol from *your* home, wait until the morning, skip that first part and start with, "Tell us what happened, how you decided to drink. Have you tried it before?" Promise there will be no punishment and that you just want to help with better decision making, and this will help you do that. Hopefully you'll get some more information here; then you can say, "I get that you are going to be in situations where alcohol and drugs will be available to you. I know we've talked to you about how dangerous starting to use this stuff is, but I also know that doesn't help in the moment when you have the booze or drugs right there in your face. That's really a hard moment. Let's try to come up with some strategies that will help you in those times."

At this point you should come up with actual scenarios where your teen might be facing this dilemma—parties, sleepovers, hang time with friends—and what to say or do to avoid feeling pressured into getting drunk or high. *"I can't! My parents drug-test me or smell my breath and check my eyes. It's like living with cops!"* Or *"I'm on allergy medication and alcohol makes me puke."* Provide a script and a way out that saves face. Most kids do things they know are wrong because they don't know what else to do. And most important, lock up everything in your house!

For many teens, though, who aren't anxious or pressured, experimenting with drugs and alcohol *is* the goal. They aren't looking for a way to get out of the situation gracefully. The reality is that even with a lot of due diligence like locking up your alcohol and calling houses to make sure that parents are home, and even with parents home, kids drink. That does not mean that there's nothing you can do or that you're completely powerless. Parents who say nothing either because they just don't want to deal with it, hate conflict, or have a "kids will be kids" attitude are sending their kids a very powerful message. Go. Do. Just don't let us find out about it. Teens who get *this* message have no motivation to set any limits on themselves. These are the teens who drink too much too fast and often find themselves passed out in a pool of vomit in someone's basement. That said, teens who get a consistently strong message that drinking can be dangerous and harmful to the brain and can put you in compromising and scary sexual situations will probably still drink too. Here's the difference: The repetitive and annoying lecture you give every time your teen leaves the house is somewhere in his brain. So yes, maybe he downs *a* beer or two, or *a* shot or two. But most likely your annoying voice in his head might save him from downing a six-pack of beer or eight shots of booze. Your boring, seemingly meaningless lectures niggle at the back of your teen's brain, and that could save his life. Please don't just give up the ship here. Everything you say or do will have purpose and meaning as long as it's said in a loving and nurturing tone. That is the key. Don't set up a challenge by saying something like, "If I find out that you use drugs or alcohol, you'll be grounded!" This kind of comment just pushes your teen to do it but not to get caught.

Your kids will make mistakes, many of them. It doesn't make them bad kids. They need to know that you're on top of this stuff, that you know that the opportunities are out there, and that you want to help them make safe decisions. Consequences such as being grounded for a weekend are fine, but don't go overboard and ground them for a month or longer. It won't work and it will just make them angry with you and shut down the communication that's absolutely the most important part of this. If they think their parents are always disappointed in them, they won't turn to you for help. And you want them to come to you. Who else is there?

the consequences of teens drinking in your home

it's always your responsibility to keep teens safe

Here's the Problem

Some parents believe that it's safer for their teens and their teen's friends to party with alcohol and drugs in their own home. Parents who subscribe to this theory believe that when teens drink at home, parents can teach them how to drink responsibly, develop good drinking habits, and keep them safe by taking away their car keys.

A study published in the *Journal of Studies on Alcohol and Drugs* compared seventh graders from the United States, which prohibits underage drinking, and Australia, where adult-supervised drinking for teens is allowed. *Time* reported, "By the ninth grade, 36% of the Australian teens had problems with binge drinking or other alcohol-related issues such as getting in fights and having blackouts, while only 21% of the American adolescents did."[1] So much for the theory that when parents "supervise" and give permission to allow teen drinking in their home, teens will become "healthier/safer" drinkers.

Why It's a Problem

First, IT'S ILLEGAL!!!! Many states have enacted social host laws that punish parents with fines and jail time when teens are found drinking in their home. Even if parents claim ignorance—either because they weren't home or they were home and didn't know (wink wink) that the 60 kids coming in and out of their house through various and sundry entrances were drinking—they're still liable

Moreover, think about the message it sends to the teens. A parent may say, "I give you permission to drink in our home so that we can keep you safe. I would rather you drink here than out in the woods." But what the teen hears is "Yay, my parents said I could drink." Teens do not distinguish between drinking at home and just drinking period! This gives your impulsive, fun-seeking teen an unintentional carte blanche to party anywhere, anytime.

Finally, and most important, allowing teens to drink in your home does not guarantee that they will be safe. Say a teen who has already partied somewhere else shows up at your house and is already three sheets to the wind. Now this individual is looking to finish out the night at your house, where drinking is allowed. It might not take much for this teen to black out and end up in a hospital emergency room. This happened to a parent over New Year's. She allowed her 16-year-old son to have a party with booze. She took the car keys away from the teens, breathed a sigh of relief that everyone would be safe, and went up to bed. Little did she know that one of the teens had passed out. Most of the kids thought he was just sleeping and left him alone. Thank God one responsible teen called 911. The teen had a blood alcohol level of .18, more than twice the legal limit. Good-bye New Year's Eve party, hello stomach pump.

Unless parents are psychic or make every teen provide a detailed medical history before they're allowed to drink in their home, they have no idea the baggage someone else's child may be bringing into their house. Perhaps one of the kids has a medical condition like diabetes and the alcohol/drugs trigger an insulin reaction. Maybe a teen is on a medication that when combined with alcohol causes a lethal reaction. These situations can be serious and potentially life-threatening. And finally, it's never another parent's right to give somebody else's child permission to use alcohol. This is an issue to be discussed between teens and their parents.

Here's the Solution

Never give your teens and their friends permission to drink at home. Teens think in black and white, and the message about drinking must be consistent and clear: "I do not want you to drink, and you're never allowed to drink in our home."

If you're a parent who has allowed kids to party at your home, it may be time to look at the reason you made this decision. Sometimes parents love hanging with their teen's friends. It's fun! I get that. I loved my daughter's friends, and we often hung out. But we never ever drank or smoked pot together! Maybe hanging out with your teen's friends, drinking, and smoking pot makes you feel younger, cool, and hip. In an adult life that can often be stressful and boring, hanging with the teens can be very appealing. This is not a healthy choice.

Perhaps you are a parent who hates conflict. When your teen comes to you with a cockamamie idea to have a party at the house, you cave pretty easily. They're good at convincing you that it's safer for them to be able to drink in the house. You buy it hook, line, and sinker to avoid a fight. This is not a healthy choice. Looking in the mirror is not always easy, but look you must. A teen's life might be at stake.

For solutions to keeping teens safe at house parties, go to Chapter 40.

1. Alice Park, "Does Drinking with Parents Help Teens Drink More Responsibly? Not Really," *Time*, April 29, 2011. Retrieved January 13, 2014, from http://healthland .time.com/2011/04/29/does-drinking-with-parents-help-teens-drink-more-responsibly -not-really/.

what happens when teens are left unsupervised

a room-for-improvement parenting story

Here's the Problem

A ninth-grade girl is "wicked" excited to be going to her first high school dance. Part of the fun is to head over to a friend's house to prepare and pre-party with a bunch of other girls. Having a daughter now grown, I have very sweet memories of these getting-ready parties. Music and mayhem followed by a parade of beautiful girls, coiffed, made up, and dressed to the nines.

Earlier in the week, the parents of this ninth-grade girl had done their due diligence, calling the host parents to confirm that they would be home supervising this dressing event and that they would be providing transportation to the dance. On the afternoon of the dance, the parents dropped their daughter off at the house thinking all was well in the world: parents home, ride to dance, done! Unbeknownst to these parents, the host parents' plans had changed. They were not going to be home and instead had left a 20-year-old nephew in charge of "supervising" and chauffeuring these wild and dance-crazy girls to the dance. The host parents had entrusted their 15-year-old daughter to relay this change to her friends, who were supposed to relay the information on to their parents.

FAT CHANCE! Huge mistake in judgment on the host parents' part. F for assuming that a bunch of teens, in party mode, would willingly tell their parents that there would now be no adult supervision at the pre-party home. No

15-year-old I know would have been honest with her parents about this lack of supervision.

Why It's a Problem

Knowing that there would no nosy parents, some of the girls brought alcohol, pilfered from their own homes. One girl in particular drank a lot, so much that by the time she got to the dance she was so drunk she fell down, vomited all over the floor, and wound up in the ER for possible alcohol poisoning. Perhaps if the person who was "supervising" and who drove the kids to the dance had noticed and interceded, then the girls might not have gone out in a compromised and potentially dangerous condition. But let's face it, the 20-year-old "chaperone" was probably thinking about his own evening plans once he dumped the girls at the dance!

The parent who told me this story felt that her daughter had betrayed her trust by not being honest that the host parents' plans had changed. But the issue isn't trust. It's *temptation*. Teens sometimes find themselves in situations that are just too good to be true, like this one. It's unrealistic to expect that an impulsive, thrill-seeking teen surrounded by giddy and excited friends will "do the right thing." In this case, the adults set up the teens to fail.

Here's the Solution

→ Do not leave teens alone in a house, especially before a major social event. If your teen is going to "pre-party" at a friend's house, make sure you communicate to those parents that if their plans should change, and they can't be home, you want to be contacted by them personally.

→ If you are hosting such an event at your home, call the other parents personally and let them know the plan. Make sure you let them know that no alcohol is allowed, and if you find any or suspect that anyone has been drinking or doing drugs, their parents will be called immediately to pick up their teen. They should talk to their kids about the alcohol issue.

→ Never ever depend on a teen to relay messages about plans like this. They are motivated to find a way to have a good time. If that means a lie of omission, so be it. They want to keep their parents in the dark. How else can they expect to have a good time!

→ Be aware of containers teens may be using to mask alcohol use. Watch for Red Bull, iced tea, soft drinks, and water bottles. Slyly ask for a sip: "Hey, I never tasted Red Bull. Can I try it?" If they hesitate or make up a story like, "Oh, I have a cold," be suspicious!

→ Lock up your alcohol. Your teens could be getting their booze from your house.

As parents, you have to understand that all this party stuff is exciting. Your teens are "living the dream" and they're impulsive, a scary combination. Your job is to anticipate possible holes in their plans, problem-solve around them, and understand that not all parents are responsible. The buck stops with you!

37 a chilling drinking story
alcohol and date rape

Here's the Problem

A group of high school sophomore girls decided to have a weekend sleep-over. They had been friends since elementary school and had remained "besties" through their middle and high school transitions—no easy feat. It had been a family lovefest; parents and kids had all known and adored one another for years. On the evening of the sleepover, the girls had all their gear piled down in the basement, like always. The parents said their good-nights around 11 p.m. and went up to their bedroom, two flights away. This group had had hundreds of sleepovers together, and so these parents went to bed free of worry that there would be any "shenanigans." After all, these were the "good girls."

Once the girls were "free," they pulled from their backpacks the "forbid-den fruit," alcohol. It seems these actually were the "good girls." None had ever been drunk, choosing to stay sober at parties for fear of embarrassing themselves. Tonight was the night. They had planned a night of drinking in a "safe house," among the friends they trusted the most, to see what being drunk felt like. Let the drinking begin.

Throughout the evening, one of the girls—the "hostess"—had been text-ing with a "hot" popular senior boy. It seems he had a girlfriend but thought this girl was cute, and he badgered her to invite him over. As this girl became more intoxicated and flattered by his attention, the conversation took a turn and she gave him permission to sneak in the basement door. Her friends had passed out in an adjacent room. That is the last thing she remembered until she awoke the next morning, dressed in different clothes, a used condom on the floor next to the couch and a feeling of soreness in her vagina and pubic area.

As you can imagine, this girl became hysterical. Thank God she had a good relationship with her parents and was able to run up to their bedroom for help.

Why It's a Problem

The problem was the lack of supervision. Because these parents had such a long history with this group of girls, they felt completely comfortable with them in the basement, away from prying parent eyes. The word these parents used was "trust." But this was not a case of a betrayal of trust. It was a case of temptation gone wrong.

Because these teens could count on the parents leaving them alone, they felt the freedom to follow through with their plan. It's wonderful to have teens in your life whom you have known since they were young children. But like all children, they grow up. With each new stage of development come new cautions and concerns. As eight-year-olds, the biggest worry at a sleepover was that they would eat too much junk food or not get enough sleep. But it's different for teens. If there is lax supervision then there is opportunity and temptation for teens to let the impulsive, awesome-seeking drives completely take over. For these girls it was the abuse of alcohol and the resulting date rape.

A really scary part of this story is the amount of alcohol these girls consumed. Three girls blacked out and one was date raped. Many teens engage in binge drinking. They take a few shots, don't feel anything, and take a few more. Maybe it's Jell-O shots, or gummy bears soaked in booze or just straight up with a juice chaser. However they do it, it's a recipe for disaster. If a little is good, more must be better. Teens do not practice patience or moderation when it comes to alcohol. Subsequently, they're at risk for engaging in extreme behaviors. Just ask this girl who lost her virginity to a random guy in her basement.

Here's the Solution

For the sleepover part of this story, the solution is supervision, supervision, supervision. When your teen has a sleepover, even if it's with kids you've known forever, you need to be a presence. As soon as they arrive, say something like, "Hope there's no booze in those backpacks. I'm like a bloodhound, I have a nose for knowing!" Before you head up to bed, you say to your party-prone overnight guests, "Hey, guys, just want to let you know that I am up and down all night. Total insomniac these days, might come down to do laundry if I can't sleep. I hope I won't keep you up" (wink wink). This lets the teens know that you will be up and around. It gives them structure and safety that will keep them from doing something they might regret. And stay up you must. Set your alarm for every hour and a half or so. And do that laundry! Parents really get mad at me for this advice, claiming exhaustion. But just remember when your teen was an infant and was up every two hours at night. I'm guessing you never said, "Hey baby, I'm tired, leave me alone!" Teens need their parents now just as much as then, maybe even more.

Tell this story to your teen. It's an excellent example of what happens when kids binge drink. This is an important lesson. Your message should always be clear: "I don't want you to drink. It's unsafe, it damages a growing brain, and it can potentially drive you into situations that can change the rest of your life, like the girl in the story. But I'm realistic, and I know that you'll be in situations where there's alcohol, and that you might choose to drink. Binge drinking is life-altering and life-threatening. We're begging you not to binge drink. We love you so much and couldn't bear it if something happened to you."

Scour the Web and newspapers for stories of binge drinking gone bad and share them constantly with your teen. This is NOT a onetime conversation. This is a conversation that should happen every single time your teen leaves your home to party with friends. Repetition is how people learn. This message has to be repeated so often that your teen can finish your sentence for you. It might become the family joke: "I know . . . no binge drinking!" But it could save a life.

38 dope, weed, pot, grass, cannabis, marijuana, hemp

they all spell trouble

Here's the Problem

Adults and pot: whatever turns you on. Teens and pot: not good.

I've recently had a number of letters from parents worried about their teens' use of pot. Some parents find out while innocently cleaning their teen's bedroom. Opening a drawer to put away their teen's underwear, they come across pipes, joints, or small baggies filled with pot. Some parents catch a whiff of the distinctive odor and confront their teens on the spot. It seems that whenever and whatever way teens are confronted about their suspected drug use, they're prepared with a defense, and they use a variety of rationalizations. Some of my favorites include: "*I can think better.*" "*I can drive better.*" "*Even the cops don't care.*" "*It relaxes me so I can concentrate better on my homework.*" "*You should be happy, at least I'm not drinking alcohol!*"

Unfortunately, this is the drug talking. That's really the point. Pot is all about distortion. Think of the 1960s. Why do you think the lava lamp was invented?

Perhaps your teen has badgered you with questions about your own drug use when "you were my age" and likes to use that in defense of pot smoking. I'm a full-disclosure-with-editing kind of person. If you were a full-out druggie back in the day and you're alive "but for the grace of God," being honest about your own lack of control and how it impacted your life negatively is a good way to go. If you were a "weekender," you can still be honest and talk about the difference between pot then and pot now. The THC content in some strains of pot today is many times stronger than in the 1970s. This makes it a much more dangerous drug, and that's important to convey to your teen.

Why It's a Problem

Adolescence is all about new experiences and experimentation. It's a cruel law of nature that tempts teens to try all sorts of new things just at a time when their brains are engaged in a major growth spurt.

Typically, when teens look and act drunk, you can bet they *are* drunk! Alcohol can be pretty obvious. You see the results in the toilet bowl (if you're lucky), or in someone's car or basement. With pot, the effects are less obvious. Teens who are stoned feel like they're in control. But pot only gives the *illusion* of control, and it interferes with an adolescent's deep-down brain development. As with all experimentation, some kids might see it as a treat every now and then, while others will begin to use more regularly. In either case it is important for parents to talk with them about it.

Let me give you a quick science lesson: The brain has receptors that just love THC, the chemical in pot. These receptors are connected to two very important parts of the brain: the hippocampus, which is responsible for memory and learning, and the cerebellum, which controls balance and coordination. In short, regular use of pot can adversely affect thinking and problem solving (the hippocampus). And it can distort the perception of light, sound, and time (the cerebellum). So much for the driving rationale . . . and the homework one too.

Teens like marijuana because it's fun, and it makes them feel different, and they don't throw up when they've had too much. Pot is especially attractive to teens because it relaxes them and mellows out their stress, and if they're someone who struggles with anxiety, pot can be a wonderful new best friend. There's nothing more uncomfortable than feeling anxious. When a teen suffering from anxiety tries pot, a love affair begins.

Here's the Solution

Talking with your teen about pot requires finesse and what I call the "power of understanding." Really it's just good old-fashioned empathy. It's important to refrain from lecturing. Instead, take a walk "in your teen's shoes." You can say to your teen, "I get how pot would be attractive to you. It makes you feel relaxed, and it's fun to be stoned with your friends." For those of you who have teens who struggle with anxiety, you can add, "I know sometimes you are stressed out, and it makes you feel relaxed and mellow. But here's what you don't know." At this point, instead of sermonizing and lecturing, download and either read this article to them or have them read it in your presence (http://teens.drugabuse.gov/facts/facts_mj2.php). This is a link to a very straightforward Q&A about pot. If you choose to lecture, your teen will probably just stop listening, thinking that he knows more than you about this particular subject. Real science is always good in this situation. I'm sure you'll get resistance here, and this is how you might handle it: "I'm worried that you don't feel that pot affects your judgment. You need to read this article and talk with us about it before we'll allow you to drive our car. It's important to us that you have the facts. If we see a change in your grades, or your ability to concentrate on getting your work done, we'll have to drug-test you every now and then. We love you and want to make sure that you don't unknowingly jeopardize your health and your future."

If you suspect your teen is using pot, it won't be easy to have the talk. Expect resistance, defensiveness, and a lot of denial. Try really hard not to get mad. This will not serve you well in helping your teen understand why this worries you so much. Information is power!

teen-proofing your home for alcohol and drug safety

looking at your home through a new lens

Here's the Problem

Remember when your teens were babies and had just begun to crawl? With that new ability to move about independently, they pursued with passion the opportunity to explore their home. This new perspective was beyond exciting.

Parents love this stage in the development of their children's natural curiosity. Wanting to encourage the study of this new world—while understanding that little fingers can get caught in cupboard doors while pursuing a study of "open and close" or an electric shock can come from poking fingers into funny little holes in the wall—parents set out to child-proof their home with all manner of devices designed to keep probing babies safe.

Teens are not so different. They have this new brain that is full of new thoughts and feelings. Like crawling babies, they are seeing and trying to understand their world from a new perspective. Not having any firsthand experience, they too are full of curiosity. *"What happens when you actually drink alcohol, not just take a sip from a parent's glass?"* *"My mom takes a pill to make it easier to fall asleep; I wonder how that makes you feel?"*

Because the frontal cortex—the thinking, problem-solving, and understanding consequences part of the brain—does not stop developing until age 22 or 23, teens are vulnerable to potential danger zones in the home. Alcohol left in refrigerators and unlocked liquor cabinets, prescription drugs left on countertops and in medicine cabinets, these can feed the beast of temptation.

Why It's a Problem

A 12-year-old boy is on his way to a sleepover at a friend's house. He gets in his mom's car with a backpack slung over his shoulder. Mom becomes a bit suspicious because her son has never taken a backpack to a sleepover before. It's not like he and his friends are going to try on different outfits like her daughter and her friends do at sleepovers. So, the mom wonders, why the backpack? She notices a bulge in the front section of the backpack and asks her son what's in there. He starts to cry, opens his pack, and pulls out two 16-ounce cola bottles filled with a blend of the brown booze he found in his parents' liquor cabinet. Do the math: That's 32 ounces of alcohol, a deadly amount for anyone. The mom who told me this story said, "Never in a million years did I think I had to lock up our alcohol to keep my 'little boy' from taking it!"

It's summer, and a group of 14-year-old teens are meeting in the woods (behind a police station; go figure) for a lazy afternoon hang. Getting kind of rowdy, they attract attention from some cops at the station. When the police approach the kids, they find a few bottles of "fine merlot." Where do you think those came from?

A 15-year-old boy has invited a bunch of buddies over for a sleepover. In the morning, after the boys leave, the mom goes down to the basement to clean up. Lying right on top of a trash basket in the adjoining laundry room, she sees a bunch of discarded beer cans. She's furious that her son has betrayed her trust by allowing his friends to take and drink the beer from the refrigerator in the laundry room. When she confronts her son about this he says, "Mom, you gotta lock up the beer. You can't expect me to say no to my friends!"

The four major issues at play here are temptation, accessibility, lack of good decision-making skills, and a hyper-sense of self-consciousness. Whether it's alcohol, mind-altering drugs, or prescription medication, many teens are tempted. Not only will teens take advantage of the bounty, but their friends will too. And in fact, friends may pressure your teen to become their "party" resource. Because teens worry so much about what others think about them, saying no to a friend who wants to score from your house is almost impossible with taunts like, "Hey man, stop being such a wuss!" or "Come on, your parents will never find out" or "You're such a loser." It's not easy being a teenager.

Eliminating the "temptations" from your home is your only solution. Sure, they may still find other means of obtaining these substances, but at least you won't be contributing, and you're sending a clear message that using and potentially abusing alcohol and drugs is serious.

Here's the Solution

You child-proofed your home in the early years. Now you must teen-proof your home for the teen years.

→ Lock up all alcohol. This includes wine cellars and basement refrigerators that hold beer.

→ Put all prescription drugs in a lockbox. I know it's a pain if you take them regularly, but that's life!

→ If your teen is on medication for ADD or ADHD, make sure that only you dole out the daily dosage. Many parents mistakenly give their teens the responsibility for managing this medication. They are not ready to do this. Many teens share this medication with their friends when they have easy access. Kids crush it and snort it for an easy high.

→ Model good drinking habits at home and when you are out with the family. Say out loud, "No drinking for me. I'm the designated driver tonight." Your teens will watch your every move now that alcohol is potentially a part of their lives. How you handle your drinking is a model for how they will handle their drinking.

Teens will definitely notice these changes and want to know why you don't trust them. Of course, they're trying to put you on the defensive and make you feel guilty for not trusting them, all in the hope that you will unlock "Pandora's box." Stay strong! Remember those electric outlets of yore! You can say, "It's not about trust honey, it's about temptation and safety.

I would never knowingly want to put you in harm's way, and I would never want to put you in the position of having to say no to a determined friend who sees available contraband. I know how hard that can be. Now you can just say, 'My stupid parents have everything locked up.'"

40 party planning with your teen
commonsense rules

Here's the Problem

Quite simply, teens love to party, anywhere, anytime. Teens are spontaneous and extremely mobile, which means that a simple tweet or text can send hordes of kids to a new party location in a matter of minutes. Parents who have "just left the building"—out for dinner with friends, for example—might return home to find a party in full swing.

Maybe you and your honey have finally found time to steal a weekend away for the first time in years, or perhaps there's a family event out of town and your kids aren't going. You have plans in place for your teens to stay with friends or family while you're away, and have said to them very clearly, "You're not allowed to come back to the house while we're away." FAT CHANCE.

Perhaps you've given your teen permission to have a party. She says that a bunch of kids are coming to hang out, no big deal. You're happy that she wants to have friends over, and because you're one of the "responsible parents," you feel your presence will keep the teens safe and well behaved. You have told your teen to let her friends know that there's no alcohol or drugs allowed. "I know, I know, they won't" is the reply.

You trust them, they're good kids, and you basically stay out of their way, watching TV up in your bedroom. Around 10 p.m. your doorbell rings. It's the police, who've received a call about a noise disturbance. Down the basement you go, only to find more than the "bunch" of kids you were expecting. There are 50 or 60 of them, bolting out the basement doors and into the woods behind your house, and you find evidence that a huge party had been happening right under your nose. Bottles, butts, and cans abound.

Why It's a Problem

Teens are crafty creatures. If they're motivated to make something happen, there is no stopping them. The only tactic parents have to combat this enthusiasm is to anticipate and prepare for any and all contingencies. In moments of "awesomeness," regardless of the rules you have set or the expectations you have shared with your teens, they are vulnerable to their own impulsivity and to the pressures from their friends. Saying things like, "You better not" or "You're not allowed; you know our rules" are not helpful to teens in the moment of decision. What they need is a strategy.

Here's the Solution

If your teen is hosting a party at your home:

→ Your teen must provide you with an approximate number of kids coming over, not to exceed 20, unless you honestly can handle more and keep them safe. A list of the names of the kids would help. This guards against kids who just show up having read a text or Twitter post about a party at your house.

→ All teens enter and leave through the front door, and leave jackets, backpacks, water bottles, and any other suspicious containers in your entry hall. This guards against kids bringing booze or drugs into your home in an obvious way. They'll still try to sneak it in; there's only so much you can do. This means if you have basement doors or back doors, you have to be vigilant, walking around the house periodically to make sure kids aren't coming in or going out without your knowledge.

→ Any teen found with alcohol or pot will have the parents called for pickup.

→ If pervasive drinking occurs, the party is terminated and parents are called.

→ If the party is in the basement, make timely walks around the house to make sure kids aren't drinking in the yard or bringing booze into the basement.

→ Teens who leave the party cannot return. (Kids like to take "walks" to get high and then return to the house.)

→ Before the party starts, "walk the perimeter" of your property. Teens will often stash their booze in bushes around the party house during the day while parents are out on errands and bring it in the basement door in the evening.

→ Be a presence during the evening. Going up to your room is a no-no. Pleading ignorance when something bad happens is not an excuse.

If you are going away for a weekend/vacation without your teens:

→ Call your local police and advise them of your plan. Let them know you have teens who are staying with friends/family and that they know that they're not allowed back to the house, but just in case you would like them to patrol your house regularly.

→ Make sure that whoever is taking charge of your teens understands that you have told them they're not allowed back to the house unsupervised. If they forgot something like clothes or homework materials, they will need to be accompanied back to the house by an adult.

→ Tell your teens that for their own safety they're not allowed back to the house without an adult. Let them know you've called the local police and they will be patrolling regularly. You might say, "I get that some of your friends will be psyched we're out of town and are hoping for a great place to party. Now you can tell them that your dumb parents have called the cops, and they're going to be all over the place. I hope this will help you get out of a tough situation."

If you're going out for the evening:

You have to trust your own gut here. If you have teens who have a few close friends, are not the partying kind, have shown little interest in partying, and are happy at home with a good video game, a friend, and some popcorn, I think you can safely go on your way, leaving them alone. If you have very social, friend-loving, partygoing teens:

→ They should know that there are no friends over while you're out. You might say, "I get your friends are always looking for places to party. You can't have friends over if we aren't home. If you just feel like hanging by yourselves tonight, that's great, but what's your plan if a friend says, 'Hey, we'll come to your house, your parents aren't home.'?"

→ Early in the day, let your teens know your plan and your time of departure. If they don't have a plan for their evening before you leave, then you should drop them off at a friend's on your way.

If your teen is going out for a night with friends and there might be drinking or drugs, you need to help with scripts and strategies to help your teen get out of situations that are potentially unsafe.

→ If your teen doesn't want to get into a car with someone who has been drinking: "Thanks, I don't need a ride. I'm going with someone else."

→ If a friend has been drinking and wants to drive: Get a few friends together and grab the keys from the kid who shouldn't be driving. Text the parent in the house that you need some help.

→ For unwanted sexual advances from someone who's been drinking: "My boyfriend wouldn't want me to fool around with anyone else."

→ When your teen is at a party but doesn't want to drink: "I'm allergic to alcohol and it makes me sick." "I feel like crap. I'm going home." "My parents drug- and alcohol-test me." "I'm in training, and my coach would kill me." "I'm on this medication, and it's really bad to drink while you're taking it."

Make an "escape plan" for when your teen is in a situation that makes him feel unsafe. Have a code word he can text. When you get that text, you'll have a plan that automatically kicks in, like picking him up around the corner from where he is.

When that unsafe situation arises, the teen should go to the bathroom—for a long time—and text you the code word.

Just when you are relishing the freedom from having to pay for a babysitter, you find yourself taking on that role yourself, as house sitter. It doesn't last forever, and keeping your teen safe and your house safe is worth the peace of mind. My advice: Have a lot of dinner parties and be the go-to party house for your friends. At least then you get to have as good a social life as your teen!

talking to your teen about sex

Here's the Problem

First, it should come as no surprise that teens like sex. This is nothing new, nothing particular to this generation. When your body talks, you just have to listen! If we're honest with ourselves, we'll remember our own steamed-up windows while parking at our town's "lovers' lane" or make-out sessions in a friend's basement. But the big difference was that it was private, between couples, and behind closed closet, bathroom, bedroom, or laundry room doors. And rarely did it include oral sex at age 13.

I don't think parents are ever prepared for that moment when they discover their kid's interest in sex. Perhaps you found an opportunity to check your teen's text messages and were rewarded by graphic, almost pornographic conversations about sex between your daughter and a boy you've never heard of. You were not a happy parent. Or perhaps you wandered into the basement where your teen and company were hanging out. You intended to offer pizza, but found yourself at a full-on make-out party. Or maybe you did your good parent deed by volunteering to chaperone your teen's ninth-grade dance and were horrified by the "grinding" going on with the couples on the dance floor. (For the uninitiated, "grinding" is basically sex standing up with clothes on.) This is not the "bear hugging" of days gone by. Or perhaps you witnessed some "twerking" going on. Think pelvic thrusts standing up in rhythm to the music. Use your imagination; it's another form of sex simulation. However and wherever you become aware of your teens' interest in sex, it pushes many buttons: worry about their reputation, worry about safe-sex issues and STDs, and worry about their age and readiness for what they may be engaging in. Finally, this realization involves truly understanding and coming to terms with having a child who's not really a child anymore, and concluding that there're many things you can't control. Sex is one of them. That can be scary and unsettling.

Why It's a Problem

Teens today engage in what I call performance sex. This is a generation that has grown up with reality shows galore, many of which make public, drunken sex a performance art. The idea of a committed couple enjoying intimacy and pleasure in privacy is so "old-fashioned." Another disturbing new development for these millennium teens is that sex is often a one-way street and less a reciprocal expression or exercise in mutual satisfaction. Girls willingly offer to give oral sex and boys freely request it. An innocent game of spin the bottle has given way to inventive and creative ways to have group sex. Take, for example, the game of "stone face." In this game a group of boys sit around a table, while girls under the table provide pleasure to the boys. The boys who are on the receiving end are supposed to stay stone face, and the game is guessing who's being serviced. Lovely. Another game is the lipstick game. Girls with different colors of lipstick perform oral sex on the same guy, thereby leaving a rainbow effect on his penis. See, there's the art part!

There are endless variations of oral sex tales. Like this true story: Some middle school kids are on a field trip. A bunch of boys are sitting in the back of the bus while girls perform on the floor below. After all, riding on a bus is soooo boring. A teacher comes back to check on the kids and imagine his surprise! Another true story: A custodian was cleaning up the school auditorium after an assembly and happened upon a seventh-grade girl and fellow seventh-grade boy engaging in oral sex. Imagine his surprise! And another: Two eighth-grade students who decide to head for the empty faculty library after school for a little tête-à-penis. They find a friend to act as lookout, but as a teacher approached he got spooked and ran away, leaving this couple for the teacher to find. Imagine her surprise! Just so you know, these are good kids, from good families and good communities. Get the message?

So what's going on here? Somehow as adults, we've missed the boat. We haven't provided our kids with a healthy alternative to what the culture and the media are heavily promoting. Because the whole idea of kids engaging in these kinds of sexual activities is so nauseating, I think we've avoided the conversation entirely and left these teens with no adult perspective and guidance.

The underlying issue here for girls is the attention of and desire for a boyfriend. Many kids I have talked to and read about in the research on this subject speak to this issue. In my day, you baked a batch of brownies for a boy you had a crush on and he got the picture. Today, offering sexual favors is de rigueur. From the boys' perspective, not much has changed in terms of motivation: testosterone and good old-fashioned, notches-on-the-bedpost competition. An especially provocative and eye-opening account of teen sexual behavior can be found in the book *Restless Virgins (Love, Sex, and Survival in Prep School)* by Abigail Jones. It's a nonfiction exposé of teen sexual behavior at a prestigious private boarding school. This is not a book for the fainthearted, but it will open your eyes to the issues so that when you do decide to talk to your teen, you'll have some factual information as a basis for discussion.

Here's the Solution

Remember your first conversation with your parents about sex? The birds-and-the-bees conversation I had with my dad at age 12 was so sweet and innocent compared to today's talk, which is more like Disney vs. Girls Gone Wild. We are WAY past talking about menstruation/masturbation and "when a man loves a woman." Today's talk requires a facility with language that you might find on 1-800-who-wants-sex.

Step 1: Get comfortable with the language of sex. For those of you who do not like saying "blow job" out loud, run to your nearest closet, close the door, and repeat a thousand times, "blow job, blow job" until you have desensitized yourself to the sound of the word in your head. This is a necessary step because once kids sense that their parents are uncomfortable with the conversation, they'll run from you, since their discomfort is worse than yours, and they will look for any excuse to escape your grasp. As long as they don't have to think or talk about sex, getting on with it feels OK. That's why these conversations are so important. They're also important because of the misinformation that kids have about sex in general. In an article, "Students Find More Sex Than Education," teens cite these factoids: *"You can't get pregnant if you have sex in water. If you have oral sex you won't get an STD. There is no point in wearing a condom because it will probably break."* It's good to know they have accurate information at their fingertips!

Step 2: The actual talk. Timing is everything. Don't just walk into their room and start in. I know I have created a ton of parent anxiety here, and your impulse is to just get it over with, but patience, patience, patience. Find an opportunity. Perhaps your teen is off to a party this weekend or at a camp reunion over the holiday break or a community ski trip. Perhaps when you are driving them to an upcoming event, you might start a conversation like this: "You must be excited about going to _____. It will be so fun to hang with everyone and celebrate." Or rent some teen movie, or watch *Gossip Girl*, or some show on TV that will be sure to have sex in it (that shouldn't be hard). Then you might say, "I was listening to a story on NPR (or on talk radio, or *The View*, or you heard it from a friend from work) about how sex is different for teens than it was when I was a teen." And with a little humor, you can say, "They were talking about all different ways to have blow job parties." Your kids may be so shocked that you have said this word publicly that they'll want to bolt at the next red light. So, with a little sarcasm, you can add, "I'm sure you and your friends never do this stuff, but have you heard about it going on?" Perhaps they may have something to share here if you have kept the conversation light. The danger is in getting too serious and shutting your kid down. You know how dogs can smell fear and take that as an invitation to become aggressive? Well so will your kids. The goal here is not to frighten, but to entice.

Step 3: You've introduced the topic, and now you can try to impart some information. Because that's what this is all about. It's not about a moral lesson. If you go for the moral lesson, I guarantee your teen will walk away. Teens don't want to be told what they can and cannot do. Remember, "you are not the boss of me" is very much in play here. If you get negative and lecture, your teen will see it as a challenge rather than a consultation. One parent I know downloaded a picture of a mouth full of chlamydia (which, by the way, is climbing at alarming rates) and said something like, "You know if someone you are fooling around with wants to have oral sex, this could be your mouth. If that happens, we could be spending some time in your pediatrician's office." If you can't find a picture, perhaps you could let your teen know just how uncomfortable the symptoms of chlamydia are. Once your child is thoroughly disgusted, you can calmly say, "I get that kids are doing stuff like this, and there must be a lot of pressure out there to be part of it, even if it isn't something you're comfortable with."

For a daughter: "I get that it's nice to have attention from a guy, especially if it's someone you have a crush on. But truly, you could just be another notch on his tally of how many girls he can get. Most guys do not want a girlfriend who's so willing to have oral sex with random guys. They'll wonder who else she does this with. Go bake him some brownies instead."

For a son: "I get that girls will probably be throwing themselves at you, but honey, what they really want is a relationship and a boyfriend. And if you ask or allow a girl to give you oral sex, you're setting yourself up for expectations from this girl that you like her and want to have a relationship with her. And if that's not the case, just say no!"

Step 4: It's important to discuss the combination of alcohol- and drug-fueled sex. Most kids would never do any of this if they weren't buzzed. I once had a parent call me and say that her daughter had asked to go to the doctor to get on birth control, just in case she got drunk one night and had unprotected sex. Now there's a conversation opener! But in truth that's not an unlikely scenario. Instead, try saying something like this to your daughter or son: "Do you really want your first experience with making love to be on a cold bathroom floor with your partner puking their guts out afterwards? Sex is a great thing, but timing and location and, most important, connection are what make sex great."

This is tough stuff. Thinking about your kids in these positions, and I mean literally and figuratively here, is traumatizing. I GET IT. But your job is to get your kids to *want* to have these conversations with you, and that takes finesse and creativity. Parenting teens is often about putting aside your impulsive need to get something through their thick heads. Your kids need your help with this, especially because they won't feel comfortable coming to you first, thinking they're supposed to know what to do. The truth is they absolutely do not know what to do. Why should they? This body of theirs is brand new—the way it looks, the way it feels, and what it does. It doesn't come with instructions, and believe it or not you're probably the only people who will give them the straight info they need. So go into the closet, get comfortable with the language, and come out again, confident and comfortable with your new role as Dr. Ruth.

No parent is ever ready to see her adorable, cuddly child turn into a sexual animal. But there's no stopping it. Embracing it and helping your teen to develop healthy, safe attitudes toward sexual behavior is as much a part of parenting as teaching kids to look both ways before they cross the street. It really can be as simple as saying to your teen (maybe after an incident you heard about involving sex or after finding a "sexting" message), "Life is about to change for both of us now that you're moving into having relationships that may include some fooling around. It's so hard for me to think of you in this way, but I love you and I'm excited for you to understand what it's like to be in a relationship in which you get to know someone else in new ways. I do want you to be able to come to me when you need help, so I'll try not to close my eyes and cover my ears and yell, 'La-la-la-la-la-la-la-la, I can't hear you!' I'll try not to judge you or criticize you for having feelings that are totally normal, and I'll hopefully help you to stay emotionally and physically safe. I know that you'll be in brand-new situations where kids might be doing stuff that you're not ready for and that makes you uncomfortable. I really can help you with that kind of stuff. At the least we can brainstorm some ways that make you feel more comfortable in those situations and some strategies for getting yourself out of them without feeling like you're making a fool of yourself. I love you and I'm excited for you, and I want you to be OK."

And there you have it. You will have opened the door to understanding that sex is a part of growing up and that you want your teens to feel that they can come to you for help and guidance, not criticism and punishment. Seeing your teen in this new body and knowing all that it entails can be scary, but showing that you embrace and accept these changes at least gives you an invitation to the party.

42
boy wants sex, girl likes boy
helping your daughter say no

Here's the Problem

A mom called and told me how upset she was about the text messages her 13-year-old daughter was receiving from a 15-year-old boy. The daughter is in the eighth grade; the boy is in the ninth. This mom is extremely proactive in monitoring her daughter's Facebook wall posts and text messaging, thank God! Her daughter knows that her mom is doing this. It's above board. Lately, the mom had been seeing Facebook messages, wall posts, and text messages from this boy asking for sex, pure and simple. When her mom talked to her after reading one of these text messages, the daughter admitted that while she was flattered by the attention of an "older boy," she was also upset and uncomfortable with his requests. Ambivalent, she'd told him to stop, but only in the mildest way.

Why It's a Problem

I understand this girl's conundrum. If she tells this boy to stop asking for sex, and she sounds like she means it, then she worries that this boy will stop paying attention to her. She likes the attention, just not the pressure about sex. This is a tough dilemma for a 13-year-old. Clearly this girl is unable to set the limit, but she has to.

Here's the Solution

Here's the conversation I encouraged this mom to have with her daughter, and an action plan to stop the sexual harassment: "I get how hard it is to tell this boy to stop sending you these kinds of text messages and posts. I know you don't want me to call his parents, so here's what we can do instead. You and I will sit down together and write a text for you to send to him. In this text, you will make it clear that your parents read your text messages and that if he doesn't stop sending you texts that pressure you about sex they're going to call his parents. Tell him to stop sending the texts and to stop posting messages on your wall. We'll then block his number on your phone, so for now he'll be unable to text you. I know you don't like this, but we need to get him to stop harassing you. Also, I want you to unfriend him on Facebook. Again, I know you kind of like this boy, but since it's so hard for you to be clear, which I understand, I have to help you do this. The only other choice is to call his parents, and I know you really don't want us to do that. I love you, and I want you to be safe. I'm not blaming you. I'm not mad at you. I just want to make sure that this boy understands that you're absolutely not interested in a sexual relationship with him."

If you are a parent of a boy, he needs some talking to. Harassing girls for sex can get him into trouble. Text messages and Facebook messages are all public. Irate parents who see these kinds of messages being sent to their daughter will react, and react harshly. Please explain that to your son, and, most important, teach him respect for women and the word "NO!"

Reading sexually provocative messages either to or from your teen is hard because you know your teen feels so much is on the line in the way she responds. It's hard because so much of this stuff sneaks by you, and that makes you worried about what else your teens are experiencing that you don't know about. Just stay alert and keep monitoring and supervising. They may hate you today, but they'll thank you tomorrow.

43

spin the bottle and other sexual situations

strategies for good decision making

Here's the Problem

Story 1: A seventh-grade girl comes home from school and tells her mom that at school that day, a 12-year-old boy—a friend, not a boyfriend—came up to her in the hall and out of nowhere snidely said, "Saw you hanging with your boyfriend this weekend. Are you gonna have sex? I mean maybe you'll have your period so you know you won't get pregnant." The parent who shared this story knows that her daughter (who does have a "boyfriend") hasn't even had a first kiss yet, let alone sex. The girl tells her mom that she'd felt upset, angry, and disgusted and that during a break at school, she'd told another male friend of hers about this incident. Wanting to defend the girl's honor, the boy corners the harasser in a stairwell and kicks him in the groin. "You better not ever say anything like that again to any girl in this school!" he says. (These kids are at an expensive private school.) On the one hand, this girl took matters into her own hands, or should we say the foot of her "male bodyguard." She felt proud of herself for "taking care of business." Do we congratulate her? She's exhibiting confidence and a "take no prisoners" approach to boys who cross the line, although maybe "You're an asshole" would also have done the trick! I'm guessing most girls wouldn't have been this assertive. Instead they would have been intimidated, humiliated, and clueless as to what to do.

Story 2: Three ninth-grade girls and three ninth-grade boys are hanging out together on a Friday night at one of their houses. The six teens are in the basement. The parents are home and upstairs watching TV. The teens decide to play spin the bottle. But instead of kisses, the boys convince the girls that when the bottle stops at them, they have to take off their tops and then their pants. The boys don't have to take off anything. By the end of the game, these three girls are sitting in their underwear in front of the three fully clothed boys. The girls report this story to a friend, and in the telling of the story, they say they just didn't know what else to do except follow the rules of the game! They didn't want to do it, but felt they had no other alternative. By the way, these are all straight A students, in honors math and science!

Why It's a Problem

It's not uncommon for parents to take on a "not my kid" attitude, especially when it comes to sexual situations. I'm guessing that the parents of the teens described in these stories truly believed that they didn't have to worry about "their" teens and sex, not yet! Therefore, these parents probably didn't spend much time talking to their teens about the situations they found themselves in. Unfortunately, this means these teens are completely unprepared and have no strategies to deal with all the sexual "firsts" that happen during the teen years.

The sexual energy that lives inside all teens' bodies could probably provide power to an entire nation. Parents need to accept that. There's no predicting when that first "spark" ignites. Since these feelings are new to them, they're not quite sure how to express them. Whatever models they have for how people deal with this explosive sexual energy will be their go-to responses. If they're watching porn, explicit sexual movies, reality TV, and provocative TV shows, it will be no surprise when they act out those scenes in their own lives. After all, reality is reality, unless someone tells them differently!

Another important factor that impedes good judgment is the adolescent's heightened sense of self-consciousness. This often interferes with a teen's ability to think rationally. He might not want to participate, but he's too worried about how other kids will judge him. In order for any strategy to be successful, it must account for these feelings of embarrassment and the need to save face.

Here's the Solution

Parents of boys: Please discuss with your sons that "talking dirty" to girls is disrespectful and unappealing to them. Not all girls will be scared. Some will run to their parents; some, like the girl in the first story, will get somebody to beat up the harasser; and some might go to an authority at the school. Getting girls to take their clothes off? No way! Here's a conversation you need to have with your son: "Hey honey, I just heard these two stories from a friend. I was so shocked. [Tell them the two stories from above.] I know that you're hanging out with girls a lot now. I know that you will potentially be in situations where there's pressure to get girls to do things, and for you to treat them in a way that I know you know isn't right. I also get that you might not know how to stop it or get yourself out of it. You can always go to the bathroom, or start looking at your phone, text us, and then say to everyone, 'My stupid parents. I just got a text from them and they have to come get me now, some emergency or something. I gotta go wait for them outside.' Or if you feel confident enough you can say, 'Hey man, enough already, this isn't cool,' which I get might be hard to do in front of your friends."

Parents of daughters: Girls need to get that boys are fearless and have no boundaries these days. The good old days when girls were treated respectfully are over. You need to prepare your girls to take care of themselves. Here is your conversation: "Hey honey, I just heard these two stories, and I was shocked. Do you think you would know what to do if you were in a situation like this? I know I wouldn't have. I get that things like this could happen when you're hanging out with your friends, and I want to make sure that you never have to do something you don't want to do just because you don't know what else to do. Let's come up with some strategies so you're not caught off guard. You can always go hang out in the bathroom and text us to come get you. You can say you're leaving and walk around the block and we'll pick you up. I know it's hard to get out of these situations without your friends thinking you're a prude, but there are ways! Let's figure some out."

There's a whole new sexual frontier out there. Teens are mimicking what the culture seems to be saying is OK to do. Turning off your TV set and not letting your teens watch R-rated movies is not the answer. Watch with them! Provide them with a counterpoint and alternatives for healthy sexual behavior.

44 keeping your teen dressing like a teen
sexy and the teenage girl

Here's the Problem

At one of my parenting parties, a mother of a 12-year-old girl asked me a question about teens dressing sexy. She described the cleavage action her daughter displays daily in her low-cut T-shirts. I resisted the urge to raise my eyebrow, hearing my own mother's voice in my head: "You're not leaving the house in that shirt, young lady." The mom felt there was nothing she could do or say about it to her daughter. After all, how could she compete against today's culture and the provocative images that abound in magazines, TV, and movies?

Why It's a Problem

This mom has a point. Open any magazine. Teenage girls are portrayed as sexy, not demure. When I was in high school, the teen fashion was kneesocks and round, collared blouses buttoned up to our necks! Virginal coeds were all the rage in those days.

Yes, your teen is getting a strong message that sexy is good. Conformity is a powerful motivator in adolescence. If "all the girls" are showing cleavage and wearing shorts that barely cover their butts, then that's what yours feels she has to do. Many teen girls don't see it as a choice. Not to dress like her friends would leave her open to ridicule and judgment. And let's not forget the attention that dressing sexy brings her way. The boys love it; she loves the boys. Case closed!

Finally, if your young teen is already dressing like a 16-year-old, she's probably also behaving like one: overly flirtatious and provocative. If she's that needy for attention, you need to figure out why. Because at 12, she's spending more time fantasizing about the future than being happy and excited about the present.

Here's the Solution

The best advice I can offer is to refrain from telling your daughter that you think she's dressing like a slut and that you absolutely forbid her to leave the house in that outfit! That merely sets up this challenge: "You think you can control what I wear? Ha! I'll just change in the bathroom at school and you'll never know!" This makes you look like an ineffective parent. Instead, you could say, "I totally understand that you're proud of your body. That's a good thing. You're a beautiful girl, and I'm so happy you like the way you look. I understand that getting attention for the way you look feels good, but I would rather see you get attention for achieving something rather than showing your cleavage. Also I know you don't get this, but wearing sexy clothes sends a message to boys that maybe you're open to not just looking sexy but *being* sexy too. This could put you in situations you might not anticipate and don't know how to handle. I love you, and I want you to be safe. I know we can find a compromise."

Remember, you control the money. When you go shopping, exercise your veto power. This doesn't mean she has to dress like a Puritan, but lots of cleavage or butt cracks at 12 are definitely a no-no. You might also go over the rules of the school. Most schools now have dress codes, and your work may already be done for you.

Your daughter will most definitely be testing the sexy waters. You can forbid her to go in, or you can go in with her, and dip your toes in together.

45 finding your teen between the sheets

love in the afternoon

Here's the Problem

It was a beautiful Sunday afternoon. The warm spring breeze flowed through the open windows, and the sunlight filtered through the blinds. The family was buzzing around doing their Sunday rituals, cleaning, organizing for the week, and doing homework. Dad walked upstairs to ask his 15-year-old daughter and her 17-year-old boyfriend, who had been "working on homework together," if they would like anything from Starbucks, as he was going on a coffee run. As he walked into her room expecting to see a bed piled high with books and notes, he was shocked to see this couple undressed and having an afternoon quickie!

Beautiful afternoon shattered. Apparently this had not been a spontaneous event. When this teen's parents checked her text messages postcoitus, they saw a carefully laid-out (excuse the pun) plan. They had hoped to have time earlier in the day when the rest of the family was gone, but the family never left. The couple, intent on commingling, was not deterred.

Why It's a Problem

Before this incident, the parents had been extremely respectful of their daughter and this relationship. Having no basement family room or semiprivate space in their home, they had given permission to their daughter and her boyfriend to hang out in her room with the door open so they might have some privacy. They had only recently given her text messaging but had chosen not to check her texts. When they finally did read the texts, they learned that the boy's parents often left them unsupervised and they were enjoying their sexual freedom in his house as well.

Questions that might be swarming around your head: How could she do this when her parents were home? How could she do this with her 10-year-old brother home, who, lacking good boundaries, often barged in on the couple? Why would she be so brazenly disrespectful to her family? And why at 15 years old is she having SEX?

Teens have sex because they want to, because they are driven to. Unless there are honest discussions with parents or other compassionate adults who might potentially offer another perspective, they don't see any downside to it.

Here's the Solution

When you see your teen in a relationship that's lasted longer than a few weeks, it's important to have a conversation. Impulsive and determined, teens are driven by their feelings, not by their brains. And with the powerful pheromones released during adolescence, they need all the help they can get. Remember, though, what you say isn't as important as how you say it. If you start a discussion that comes off as a lecture or as laying down the law—"You're not allowed to have sex!"—it will probably backfire. If you show understanding and provide some rules you can control, you might have a better outcome.

"I get that you're in a relationship. I'm excited for you. Having someone in your life who really cares for you is amazing. I also get that you guys are really attracted to each other and may be thinking about having sex. Once you get on that train, it's hard to put the brakes on, so I want to make sure you take the time to really think about it. You're only 15 and have many relationships ahead of you. If you start having sex this young, there's the potential of having many sexual partners. That means more potential for hurt when relationships don't work out after you have been so intimate with each other. There's also greater potential for STDs or pregnancy. You need to consider things like that. Also, we're not comfortable with you having sex at such a young age. We can't stop you, but you need to know we don't think it's healthy at this point in your life. So here are a few rules. Now that you have a boyfriend [or girlfriend], you may not have him [her] in your bedroom; you may not have him [her] here when we're not home, and I'll speak to the parents to let them know that we expect them to provide supervision when you're at their house. I know that you guys will be 'fooling around,' but we hope that you can keep intercourse off the table. I know that you'll be respectful of your younger sibs and us, and try not to put us in awkward situations. We love you and just want you to be safe."

Honestly, there isn't much more you can do. If they want to have sex, they'll have sex! If you have a daughter, you should consider getting her birth control. Yes, you're giving a mixed message: *Don't have sex! But if you do, you should be responsible and have birth control.* You have to acknowledge and respect their relationships and continue to offer your perspective in a way your teens might be open to hearing. You're setting limits in your home, anticipating situations your teens might find themselves in. Keep the communication open, and keep the bedroom doors open!

46 is your teen gay/lesbian?
discussions on sexuality

Here's the Problem

It's hard enough getting your head around the idea that your teen has an interest in sex. But for some parents there's an additional question of whether their teen is gay or lesbian. This can be even more overwhelming. Luckily we live in a culture now that's working toward acceptance and support for people with alternative lifestyles. But for many parents, that acceptance is easy for everyone except their own children.

Perhaps you grew up in a family where being gay was considered a sin. Or maybe you don't know anyone who is gay outside of celebrities, and it's a lifestyle that makes you uncomfortable. Maybe your worries about having a gay or lesbian child are for your teen's own safety and well-being. No one wants to see the children they love being hurt or excluded at a time of life when kids can be very cruel.

A couple I worked with found some "love letters" in their 15-year-old daughter's room to and from another 15-year-old girl in her class. Shocked, worried, upset, you name it, they became obsessed about this relationship. They scoured their daughter's texts, journals, and Facebook to see if this was a "real" relationship. There seemed to be a lot of drama between the two girls, and the parents worried that this would spill out at school and that the other kids would find out about them and make their lives a living hell. After all, this is high school, and the whole sexual awakening thing is brand new to all of these kids. The parents knew that anything different or out of the ordinary can feel extremely threatening. And it scared them silly.

Terrified and uncomfortable, they were unsure of how to handle this new information, and to this day they have yet to talk with their daughter about it. They supervise sleepovers and try to limit the time the girls spend alone together, but they worry if they bring it up to her, it will drive her more into the arms of the other girl. They are in pain.

Why It's a Problem

As a teen's body awakens for the first time, it can feel like a flood. There are uncontrollable feelings, sensations, and attractions. Their brains don't keep up with their biology, and often the physical and emotional get all tied up in one package. Maybe this young girl is gay, maybe she isn't. But what I can say for sure is that she's having feelings and sensations she's never had before. She has no experience with them, doesn't understand them, and isn't processing them. And, like any new relationship—heterosexual or homosexual—there can be a lot of drama. These are emotionally vulnerable young people who are in need of some adult guidance to help them sort out their feelings and their sexuality.

Sexual identity is an ongoing process that may begin before adolescence. Part of that process is to experiment with different kinds of intimacy, both physical and emotional. That's a powerful combination.

Here's the Solution

If, like the parents in the story, you have found clues that lead you to have some questions about your teen's sexuality, it's important to have an open conversation. Teens are like dogs. They can smell your anxieties and worries. Instead of coming to you for help, their worry for you will make them keep all their own worries to themselves. And if they've heard you make disparaging remarks about gays and lesbians, they'll obviously feel that you already have an opinion on the matter and they definitely won't come to you for help.

Opening the door to discussion is going to be awkward. But you know what? Sexual discussions in general are awkward, so just acknowledge it and own your discomfort. You might start this way: "Honey, I was cleaning your room last week, and you left some letters on the floor. I assumed they weren't private and read them. [Expect anger about privacy here.] I get that you feel we violated your privacy, and obviously this is uncomfortable for you, and honestly it is for us too. No one wants to talk to their parents about sex, and this is harder because it seems you are having a relationship with a girl [or boy], and that is something that caught us off guard." [It is so important for you to appear nonjudgmental even if you are not feeling it. Anything in your voice that sounds like you think there is something gross or disgusting about it will shut your teen down, and you do not want that to happen.] I know you and she [he] are really close friends. She [He] is someone you can really share your feelings with, and that's wonderful. It sounds, though, like your friendship is moving in a physical direction. That does concern us. It would concern us if you were moving in that direction with someone of the opposite sex as well. How you choose to express your sexuality is your business. We love you and just want to make sure that the decisions you make now will be decisions you'll feel good about later. Now please tell us about the relationship."

It may be that your teen is leaving not-so-subtle hints—either through actions or conversations—just waiting for you to notice the obvious. So notice away! "Honey, recently you've made some comments, and I'm wondering if you're gay."

Maybe you have a teen who has not yet opened the door for conversation, and as a parent you're not sure what to do. You don't want to ask outright, "Are you gay?" It could be too scary for him to actually say the words out loud to anyone, let alone you. Leaving hints about your own feelings of acceptance would be comforting. Maybe you have a family friend or colleague who has a gay son or daughter. You might say, "I saw Sam the other day and met his boyfriend. I'm so happy for them. They seem really happy. I know he had a rough time when he was a teen dealing with his sexuality. Seeing him so comfortable with himself and his partner is wonderful." At the least, your teen hears that being gay is OK with you.

Depending on what you hear, you can offer to help your teen get in touch with a counselor to talk with. You should contact Parents, Families and Friends of Lesbians and Gays (PFLAG.org) for information and support for families of gay and lesbian youth.

The bottom line is you can't control your child's sexual identity. I understand that some parents have a philosophical or religious point of view regarding homosexuality. You can own that and how it relates to you and your own sexuality, but it won't apply to your son or daughter because they're not you! Loving your children means loving all of what makes them who they are, even and especially when they're not like you.

47

the consequences of sexting
a "weinergate" moment

Here's the Problem

I'd like to thank former New York congressman and former New York City mayoral candidate Anthony Weiner for helping us open a discussion about the dangers of sexting. In 2011, he sent racy photos to young women who followed him on Twitter. After the photos and the accompanying tweets were discovered and made public, he had to resign from Congress. Subsequently, he was caught doing it again, scuttling his bid for the mayor's office. It's hard enough to say to your teen, "Don't text or post inappropriate pictures of yourself on your smartphone or Facebook, Twitter, or Instagram because it can get you in trouble." Most likely your son or daughter will look at you with the blank stare that says, "Everybody does it, it's no big deal, and I don't want to talk to you about it." But thanks to Mr. Weiner and his desire to show women his manliness, and the resulting public humiliation and job loss, we now have a pretty powerful example of the consequences of sexting. For your teens, these consequences might include getting kicked out of school or off an athletic team, loss of potential jobs, internships, or admittance to college, not to mention major embarrassment.

Why It's a Problem

There couldn't be a better teaching moment than this. Here's a well-respected, smart man who's become the laughingstock of the country. He's lost the respect of his colleagues, his constituents, his family, and his friends. Honestly, the pictures weren't even that bad. He wasn't posing naked, just manly. But when the photos and sexting messages got into the wrong hands, they wreaked havoc.

Teens like to show off. The part of the adolescent brain that is in highest activation is the amygdala, the "feeling" center. Unlike adults, whose brains live mostly in the frontal cortex, or "thinking" center, teens just don't think things through. Charged up by the awesomeness of their own actions, they don't consider the possible consequences. Even if they do have a passing thought that this "just isn't right," they truly believe that they're invincible. And this is what drives teens to experiment with risky behavior. Unfortunately, many do "get away" with things they know they shouldn't be doing, and this serves to feed those feelings of invincibility. This is why it's so important for parents to take their heads out of the sand and not get caught up in the "not my kid" state of mind.

Here's the Solution

Many parents live from crisis to crisis instead of anticipating that "Yes, my kid might be tempted to send a sexy photo or text." Your first job is to acknowledge that you have a teenager who can be impulsive and has the potential to do things that are crazy, scary, and upsetting to you. This does not make your teen a bad child. It just makes you a smart parent. Would you have expected a politician to do something so risky or stupid as to jeopardize his marriage, his job, and his reputation? I rest my case.

Now that you're looking at your teen more realistically, you can move into prevention mode rather than crisis mode. Go online and find those Weiner photos or articles about them. Find a time when it seems your teen might be open to a conversation. Timing is everything. Perhaps you can catch him in a moment of lounging on the family room couch, or you could even bring the subject up at the dinner table for discussion. Show the photos and talk about the consequences of this seemingly benign action. You can say, "I get that this guy was just having fun, and obviously not worried about the potential of future harm. Boy, I'll bet he was surprised. What a turn his life has taken. How sad that such a talented, smart guy, who really loves his country and wants to serve it, was taken down by a photo. I know this seems pretty removed from your life, but it isn't. Anything you send on your phone and on Facebook, Twitter, or Instagram is public. If you choose to put up racy photos, they can come back to haunt you. Coaches, colleges, employers, friends, and parents are all potential audiences. Is it so much fun that you would risk it all? Ask Mr. Weiner."

48

a teenage girl's painful lesson

a private photo goes public

Here's the Problem

It may seem like only yesterday that your biggest problem with your teen's having a cellphone was ripping it out of her grabby little hands so she could go to sleep without it. Today, it's the newly discovered thrill of using a smartphone to take naked photos, send texts about oral sex, or have phone sex at bedtime. You probably never anticipated that your daughter would be using her phone in this way. The only training or initiation you might have had with her about her new phone was how to actually use it (and more than likely, she picked that up quicker than you did). I'm guessing you never had a conversation about sending provocative photos or language, how quickly things can get out of hand, and what the consequences could be. I'm betting you didn't let your teen know that once she pushes the send button, she has lost control over anything and everything she's shared with other people. But why would you? You were just so happy to have a dependable form of communication between you and your teen, naively thinking that the phone would be used for checking in with you and for having stupid conversations with friends. After all, that's how we adults use it! The following story is, I'm sorry to say, not rare.

Why It's a Problem

A 14-year-old girl decided to go into her bathroom, take off her clothes, and aim the camera on her phone into the bathroom mirror so she could take a photo of herself naked. Feeling satisfied with the photo, she sent it off to her "boyfriend." I use this term loosely; middle school romances have the shortest shelf life of any relationship known to mankind. Days later, the boyfriend broke up with this girl, after which he showed the naked photo of his now ex-girlfriend to a friend of his, who just so happened to be the ex-friend of the girl who took the picture. This girl, having felt slighted by the first girl, then sent the photo and the following text to every one of the contacts on her phone: "Ho alert! If you think this girl is a whore, then text this picture to all of your friends."

As you can imagine, the photo spread like wildfire, not only through this middle school but also to the other middle schools in this suburban town. The story gets worse. Every one of those kids passed the photo on to all their friends. And it just kept on going. Fortunately, somewhere along the line, parents who had been monitoring their kid's texting saw the photo and contacted the authorities. They traced its origin to the ex-boyfriend and ex-friend, who ended up being led out of school in handcuffs and into juvenile detention. Their future is unclear. There have been many mediation sessions with all involved, but for the girl who had a picture of her naked body streamed out there and beyond, it will never be over. Deciding to switch schools to start fresh, the girl was recognized as the one in "that" photo, and it started all over again.

This is scary stuff. Three young teens' lives have been forever changed. If I've said it once, I've said it a hundred times: Teens *do not* think through consequences. They live in the moment. And if the moment is awesome, and no one has drummed it into their heads that sending naked photos to a cast of thousands is illegal, immoral, hurtful, and life-altering, they will just keep on doing it.

Here's the Solution

Your kids need to hear this message over and over and over, using stories like this one (which you should feel free to use; say you heard about it from a friend at work or the gym), newspaper articles, and, most important, monitoring. Forget the issue of trust. This is not about trust or privacy; it's about temptation and safety.

It's most important for you to open communication with your teen. If you start the conversation by being judgmental and critical—"If I ever catch you sending these kinds of photos, I'll take your phone away for life. This girl is nothing more than a slut!"—you'll definitely NOT get a conversation started. You want your teen to know that you understand that it's not unlikely that kids find themselves in these kinds of situations.

You might start by saying something along the lines of "I get why this girl sent the picture. She was hoping her boyfriend would like her better and think she was hot. I get why the ex-boyfriend showed it around. He's a boy and proud of the fact that a girl sent him a naked photo of herself. COOL! And I get why the ex-friend thought it would be funny to send it out world-wide. She just wanted to get back at her former friend; that's one vindictive girl! I also get that this could happen to *you*. I know you like boys [or girls] and the attention they might pay to you. I need to make sure that you don't unknowingly get yourself into a situation that could end up like any of these kids'. Maybe you have a crush on someone or are mad at one of your friends, and you might do something without really thinking it through. My job is to help you with this stuff. So for now, every now and then I'll ask to look at your texts and photos. I get that this will feel invasive. I really won't read them that carefully; I just want to make sure there's nothing that's sexual, threatening, or hurtful. I love you and I want to make sure you're safe. If the photo you want to send is not something you would do or say in person, it doesn't belong on your phone."

Remember, just saying, "You'd better not have any sexy photos or texts on your phone" is not a strategy. Kids learn through repetition. You can't have the talk and expect they will get it. They have to be reminded constantly. Don't be deterred when your teens tell you that you're boring and stupid. Somewhere in that brain of theirs you're making a dent.

If your teen has already had the unfortunate experience of "getting caught" like the girl in the story, yelling and expressing your disgust and disappointment will not open a conversation. Your teen's shame will probably turn into anger, toward you of course. She'll shut down, making it impossible to help her learn for the future. Instead, your conversation should go something like this: "I get how humiliating this must be for you. I know you liked this boy and wanted to get his attention. Can you help me understand how you decided to take the picture, and what you hoped would happen if you did?"

Staying calm and supportive will hopefully give you some new information that will help you strategize with your teen for future crushes. You will also need to help your teen reintegrate into school, knowing that she may now be the target of salacious gossip. Teens love a good juicy story. Give her some phrases she can use when she gets comments and looks from other kids. Better to have her say in a kind of sarcastic tone: "God, I can't believe I was so stupid" or "I know, what was I thinking?" When teens own their behavior it gives other kids less to say, and they'll just have to move on.

Most important, your job is to understand that this does not make your daughter a bad person or a disgusting slut. It should be a wake-up call for you. Your teen is looking for attention and needs to learn the right way to get it. Sending naked photos, not so good; being funny, paying someone a compliment, becoming proficient in a sport, or drama, or art, or babysitting, much better.

49 sexual harassment
sending sexy photos
is not always a choice

Here's the Problem

What teenage boy doesn't like a photo of a naked girl? In the old days, teenage boys could only find photos of naked girls by confiscating taboo girly magazines from older siblings or perhaps their dad's stash. The search for these magazines was almost as much fun as looking at the actual images. Not so in today's world of smartphones and the Internet. If boys want to see photos of naked girls, they can easily access them online, or for even more fun, on their smartphones and, if they're lucky, from girls they actually know and think are hot! Some teen girls, willingly and happily, will send salacious photos of themselves to boys they like or have crushes on. But many girls are horrified at the idea of sending such photos to boys and find themselves in situations they have not anticipated and for which they're completely unprepared. Here's a situation I encountered in my coaching practice.

The parents of a ninth-grade girl were horrified when they learned that a naked photo of their daughter was circulating throughout her school. In their wildest dreams they had never imagined such a situation.

Apparently a boy from her class had approached her at school and said, "I want you to send me a naked photo of yourself." The young girl was horrified and refused. The boy continued to tease and cajole the girl daily to send him the photo. The girl continued to say, "No way!" The boy, upping the ante, told her, "If you don't send me the photo of yourself naked I'll start a rumor that you slept with me and all my friends, and that you're a slut." Nice guy.

This girl now had a decision to make. Was it better to just send him the damned photo or be faced with being called a slut? I personally would have gone with the slut option, but that's just me. This young girl decided to go with the naked photo option. Of course, the photo went viral. The ninth-grade boy, so excited to share his conquest of this girl, couldn't wait to share the image with everyone on his contact list. Humiliation ensued as the picture made its way around the school. When it came to the principal's attention, the parents were called in. Their daughter was so damaged by this situation that she was removed from school and enrolled in a private school, where she could get a fresh start.

Why It's a Problem

Here's the question I bet you are asking yourselves: Why didn't this girl go to her parents for help? Here's why. If this were your child, wouldn't your first instinct have been to call the school immediately and make your daughter tell you who the boy was, and then threaten legal charges against the school, the boy, the boy's family, and anyone else you could think of to protect your daughter? I would have.

Here's the dilemma this girl faces: If she goes to her parents, they'll go crazy and she'll become a pariah in her school. To her, this may seem like a worse option than if she just sends the guy a photo. After all, the boy *promised* that no one else would see it. The sad part is, she would probably be right, except that she became a pariah anyway. This is a lose-lose situation for a girl.

Part of adolescent brain development is a sense of hyper-self-consciousness. This new awareness can interfere with rational thinking, as happened with this girl. In her mind, fear of what her peers might think of an untrue rumor outweighed the disgust of sending a naked photo of herself to a boy who had promised to keep the picture private. Now *that's* irrational thinking.

Here's the Solution

How do we protect our kids from situations like this or prevent the situation from happening in the first place? The most effective strategy is to

BLOCK THE PICTURE-TAKING CAPACITIES ON YOUR KID'S PHONE! If your teen doesn't have a smartphone yet, this is the perfect solution. If your teen can't take a picture through her phone, then this solves the problem. With smartphones, however, this is not an option. Of course if they could just tell the boys to stick it, that would have been my best advice. For most teens, though, the vulnerability they feel interferes with the confidence to stand up for themselves.

Here's how to prevent a situation such as this from happening. First, share with your teen the story about the ninth-grade girl. As you start your conversation with your daughter (I'll get to your son later), refrain from getting in a lecture mode about self-respect. That will be a conversation stopper. You might say something like, "This poor girl, what an awful situation to be put in. I get it must be hard to know what to do; these guys can be pretty persistent. I'm guessing this girl wouldn't go to her parents because who knows what they might have done. Honey, just in case this should ever happen to you, I want you to know I won't go crazy and call the police or school. If I can help you get out of this situation before it happens, then we will have prevented this disaster from happening at all. So I promise, we'll figure out a way together for you to save your reputation and avoid embarrassment. Just talk to us."

If you have a son, here's your conversation: "I get that there might be a time when you and your friends think getting and pressuring girls to send you sexy photos would be awesome. And that when you're with your group of friends, it would be hard to say anything that might make you look like a wuss, like saying that pressuring girls to send nude photos of themselves is disrespectful. I just want you to know that once that happens and photos have been received from a girl and passed on, you're part of it. You're now open to charges of disseminating child pornography and can be arrested. If someone leaves their phone on the kitchen table, or in the school cafeteria, or on the sink when they go in the shower, and someone picks it up and looks at pictures and texts and your name or contact is anywhere in that mix, you are implicated. And besides the obvious legal ramifications, IT'S JUST WRONG!"

Who knew that smartphones would become mobile *Penthouses* and *Playboys*, using our sons and daughters as their models? Prevention is the best protection. Your job is to educate and prepare your kids for situations for which they have absolutely no experience.

Encouraging your kids to come to you before a situation gets out of control is the ultimate goal. Let them know that you'll promise to stay calm in the face of chaos.

skyping, sexting, and exotic dancing
the allure of a live audience

Here's the Problem

Okay, so this girl is not working at a local strip club, but I think I've gotten your attention. I received the following letter from a parent: "We recently discovered our 10th-grade daughter Skyping, chatting with, and dancing for the viewing pleasure of an 11th-grade boy from her school. The dancing had a very sexualized aspect to it and the discussion on the chat involved the boy masturbating while she danced."

How about reading that letter before you've had your morning coffee? Before you roll your eyes and are grateful you haven't found your daughter behaving in such an undignified manner, you should know this is definitely not the first letter or request for help I've received on this topic.

Everyone wants to be a star these days, and with the availability of computers with built-in cameras and smartphones with video capacity, and applications like SnapVideo and who knows what will come out in the next minute or two, everyone can be. Ask me, I have a bunch of videos up on YouTube. (I do not dance in any of them.)

Why It's a Problem

This particular 10th-grade girl is a straight A student, star athlete, and all-around great kid. Not exactly the profile of the kind of girl one would expect to be caught in this situation. But that's exactly the point. There really is no "that kind" of kid. Teens feel sexy, and they look for opportunities to play out what they think are sexy scenarios. In my day, we mostly fantasized about them, but in this day there are a variety of tools that kids can use to act out these fantasies, and for the most part nobody has told them not to do it. Why? Because few parents would even think that they had to. But guess what? YOU DO! Additionally, for most teens, "sending sexy," whether in photos, videos, or in texts so colorful they could be from a phone sex line, feels safe. They are removed from having to experience someone's live reaction to their display. Therefore, they never experience any shame or humiliation in the moment. It's a private moment between a teen and his or her device. Would these same kids do a striptease in front of a group at a party, or walk up to a boy or girl and ask for or offer to give oral sex. No way! But typing that or making a video that simulates it, you bet!

These are the kinds of videos that can get kids in trouble. First, there's the shame aspect. Maybe not in that moment when the camera is filming, but a few weeks later when her video has made the rounds of the boys' locker room. Second, when the boy asked the girl (or she offered) to dance, she was not thinking of consequences such as her parents finding out. No, she had the devil of impulsivity sitting on her shoulder, encouraging and cheering her on. You can thank the overactive amygdala, the feeling center of the brain, for that! She was thinking of consequences all right, but they weren't the ones that frontal-cortex-thinking adults might be having. No, here are the consequences that drove this teen: "If I dance around in my bra and panties, will he think I'm sexy and beautiful?"

Here's the Solution

It's fortunate these parents were monitoring their daughter's texts and computer use and discovered her penchant for exotic dancing and sexually charged texts. Otherwise their daughter, feeling safe from detection, may have gotten herself into some serious trouble. Now at least there's an opening to have a frank and honest conversation and discussion about dancing for boys in a sexual way and writing sexually provocative texts. Finding opportunities for conversational teaching moments is the key to successfully parenting a teen. Of course, as the parent, when you "catch" your teen behaving in a way that makes you want to lock her in a convent or monastery, you have to have a consequence, like limiting computer use to family common spaces in the presence of responsible adults, and disabling picture and video capacity from your teen's phone, if you can.

But more important is the conversation. And by the way, absolutely do not open with, "How could you do such a disgusting thing?" It's not a conversation starter. But this "I get it" moment is: "I get that you like getting attention from boys. We all like getting attention; that's totally normal. But when you make videos of yourself in a way that gives off the 'I'm here to give you sexual pleasure' vibe, that's very dangerous. Just because you think you're just having fun doesn't mean boys think that way. Boys are probably thinking that if this girl dances like this for me and sends me sexy texts, I can get her to do anything for me. Honey, this is not safe, and I don't think that you really want to be sending that message. We love you, and we want you to be safe. Help us to understand what's going on here."

Parents who have told me about these situations are surprised that their kids just don't understand why this is all such a big deal. Their teens say, "It was just fun," with no embarrassment or shame. Don't be surprised if you get the same response. But please don't wait to have this conversation until your teen gets caught. Anticipate and understand that girls and boys can get themselves into these kinds of situations and have no idea of how to handle them. Have a conversation about having respect for oneself and practicing "sexual safety" *before* something happens.

51

the legal
consequences
of sexting

my son, the sex offender

Here's the Problem

A teenage girl has a crush on a teenage boy. Unsolicited, the girl sends a photo of herself naked to the boy's cellphone. The boy receives the photo and promptly sends it to all his friends. A few days later, while at lunch in the cafeteria, the boy forgets his phone and leaves it on a cafeteria table. After lunch, the principal comes through on his daily reconnaissance, picking up jackets, notebooks, and cellphones left behind by forgetful teens. In an attempt to find the owner of the phone, the principal looks through the photos. Imagine his surprise when he finds the photo of one of the school's female students naked. Further investigation finds a text message in which this picture was forwarded to a number of boys in the class. The police are called and the owner of the phone is identified. This teen is arrested and convicted of disseminating child pornography, and he is not allowed anywhere near children for 18 years!

An 18-year-old high school senior boy, who's been in a long-term relationship with his girlfriend, just for fun decides to send her a photo of his erect penis. Joking around with his best friend one day, he shows him the photo he had sent to his girlfriend. A few weeks later, the boys are hanging out together. The owner of the penis photo goes to take a shower, leaving his phone on the desk. The best friend spontaneously picks up his phone, finds the penis photo, and decides to write a funny caption and send it to everyone on his friend's phone contact list. Ha ha ha, don't *you* think that's hysterical? NOT. The penis photo guy was in a leadership position at his high school, where he participated on many committees and worked with the principal and faculty on a number of school betterment projects. Because he regularly texted these individuals, they were on his contact list. Needless to say, when the principal and faculty members saw a text from their favorite student, they opened it, only to find this photo. [Insert gasp here!] The consequence of this X-rated texting moment was that he was banned from walking at his high school graduation. Unfair or not, his fault or not, these are serious consequences.

Why It's a Problem

Imagine being the boy in the first story. A girl sends you a naked picture of herself. It would be hard to believe that a boy of this age, or any age for that matter, would stop and say, "Oh, this is inappropriate, I'll delete this immediately from my phone." NO, this boy is beyond excited, thinking, "Oh my God, I have a photo of a naked girl on my phone. Man, I have to show my friends." Believe me, there is no rational thinking going on at all. He has forgotten all about the girl as a real person or that by sending this picture to all his friends, he's breaking the law. He doesn't even know there is a law! Maybe you didn't know there was a law either. After all, this kid isn't a pervert, just a normal, healthy teenage boy.

Imagine being the high school senior in the second story. A stupid friend and a stupid photo tainted your reputation.

It's that "awesome" part of the brain at work again. And since these teens weren't schooled in the legal ramifications and other serious consequences of sending naked photos, the thinking part of their brains cannot counter these impulses.

Here's the Solution

Think about what teens have to do before they get their driver's license. They have to read the little blue book with all the road rules and take a test on it. They have to go to driving school, where they sit in a class and talk about safe driving. They have to take driving lessons with a certified driving teacher. And finally, they have to drive with you sitting next to them giving a blow-by-blow account of what they're doing right or wrong. Smartphones can be as dangerous to kids as driving. Just ask the 12-year-old who can't be around children for the next 18 years, or the senior who was not allowed to walk at his high school graduation.

You need to give your teen cellphone lessons. You need to plant the seeds of rational thinking so that when the impulsive brain wants to hit the open road at 100 miles per hour, the rational brain kicks in. *"Hey, that's way over the speed limit."* All the stories I share in this book are to be shared with your teens. Please don't say you got them from a "parenting book." That will be the kiss of death. You might say, "I was at work today and my colleague told me this story about one of his son's friends. Did you know that sending sexual photos is illegal? I know it's hard to think of naked photos of people you know as pornography, but they are. I know it's hard in the moment when you send certain photos of yourself, or if a girl sends you a photo like that, to say to yourself, 'Oh, I'd better not send this to my friends.' But that's exactly what you have to do. Let's figure out what you can do if this should ever happen to you."

Here are some options to share with your son:

→ Let him know you will be monitoring the pictures on his phone at random times to make sure there is nothing on there that is sexual.

→ Coach him to text back to the girl, "My parents check my phone; don't send photos like this. I don't want you to get into trouble; my parents are really nosy."

→ Coach your son to delete the photo immediately, before sending it on to anyone. Remind him that other parents monitor their kids' phones and if they find a photo of a naked girl they'll want to know how their kid got ahold of it. And as the sender of the picture, he will be the one who will get in trouble . . . serious trouble.

Understand that your teen will be in situations he has never been in before and has no idea how to handle them. In those impulsive, awesome moments, damage can be done. Don't wait for the call from the principal.

52 cellphone/smart-phone monitoring
should I or shouldn't I?

Here's the Problem

When I suggest to parents that they need to monitor their teen's texts from time to time, I'm usually met with tremendous resistance. Some parents have made the decision to respect their teen's privacy. Their rationale? When they were teenagers and kept diaries or notes from friends, they absolutely did not want their parents to read them. In fact, they took great pains to hide them in secret and hard-to-find places, like under the mattress! (Of course, that's the first place any nosy parent would look.) Their diaries were personal—filled with fantasies and dreams. If what they wrote was taken out of context, their parents would flip out. The humiliation of having their parents read these innermost thoughts would be too hard to bear. Now, as the parent of a teen, they have chosen to give their teen the gift of privacy.

Other parents report to me that they're afraid to monitor their teen's texts because it might make their teen mad and they don't want to be accused of violating privacy. I get that incurring the wrath of an angry teen can be a deterrent! And finally for many parents, ignorance is bliss. Avoiding the problem means not having to deal with the messiness of what they might find.

Just ask this mom of a sweet, lovely, 14-year-old girl who came to me for help. One evening she walked into her daughter's room to put away clean laundry. The daughter, now in the shower, had left her cellphone on the desk, and her emails were up on the computer screen. This was a "respectful" mom who had never checked her daughter's phone or computer. But there they were, emails in plain sight, oh, the temptation. It wasn't like she was sneaking anything. Let the reading begin! Mom was shocked, reading a discussion between her daughter and her daughter's boyfriend regarding their recent foray into new sexual territory. They were having intercourse! Mom was horrified. She thought this relationship was just cute puppy love and had often allowed them to be in the house alone and unsupervised. So much for puppy love, and so much for privacy! Mom goes for the cellphone, and to her dismay begins reading months of texts between the two lovers that were filled with such explicit sexual language that it literally nauseated her.

Why It's a Problem

Comparing diaries of the past to today's communication tools is like comparing horse-drawn buggies to electric cars! Diaries were not two-way conversations between impulsive, suggestible, attention-seeking, sex-starved teenagers. Teens of today are completely desensitized to what they're writing and sending to one another. They don't feel the shame of being sexually provocative because they are removed from experiencing their "audience's" reactions. I highly doubt that your teen daughter would do a striptease in front of a group of boys at a party. That would be "slutty." But she might not think twice about sending a sexually suggestive photo from her phone. I also doubt that your son or daughter would use words so coarse that they are unprintable here when having an in-person conversation with a member of the opposite sex. But in a text, how fun!

Teens, especially the younger ones, have no clue what they are doing when they send raunchy photos and racy texts peppered with promises of sexual favors. They see it all as a joke, until something bad happens.

Perhaps intercourse was never really on the table for this 14-year-old girl, but after months of sexting there are going to be expectations. Enough already with the written words of titillation, let's do the real thing. When a girl offers up oral sex, or a boy requests it in a text, that boy has expectations about what the girl will do for him. Because teens are impulsive and don't think before they act, they can get themselves in the kind of trouble that can have lifelong implications and consequences.

Many teens don't like sexting, but they do it anyway, worried that if they don't respond in a way that's expected of them, they'll be judged as losers. Teens are extremely conscious about what other people think of them. This can be a powerful motivator in your teen. Here is an example: A 12-year-old boy is watching TV with his mom. He is also texting away on his phone. Mom was OK with that since her son is quite shy, and she was happy to see him texting and being social. He goes to take a shower and leaves his phone on the coffee table. (Note to teens: Showers can be hazardous to your health.) Mom picks up the phone, curious to see with whom he's been texting. It's with a girl from his class. Girl: "What's up?" Son: "I'm jacking off!" WHAAAAT! The mom is beyond shocked. When confronted about this text, the young teen starts to cry. Here's my explanation to the mom: This boy is new to the party of texting. He's heard that if you want girls to like you, you're supposed to talk dirty. He wants girls to like him, so he'll talk dirty. And jacking off is the dirtiest thing he can think of.

Additionally, boys, buoyed by watching extremely explicit porn on their computers, iPads, and smartphones, have become more brazen than ever about pressuring girls for racy pictures and sexual favors. Girls, wanting to please the boys, get a boyfriend, feel sexually powerful, or to be "popular," either offer or are pressured into providing these photos and "talking dirty."

Here's the Solution

Monitoring your teen's phone is a necessary evil. It's uncomfortable and can make you feel like a nosy parent. But understanding that harmless conversations can turn into harmful consequences should be motivation. Thank God both of these parents are now clued into their teens' worlds and can help them navigate. You can say, "From time to time you and I together will check the texts and photos on your phone. I get that this feels like an invasion of privacy, but I need to know that the conversations you're having and the photos you're getting and receiving are safe. I get that kids like to talk dirty and send sexy photos, but that's not acceptable on your phone. I don't want to see conversations about oral sex or penises or boobs."

It is important to be blunt and honest with your kids. They need to hear the words out loud. It will make them sick to hear *you* say them, and that's exactly what you want. It takes all the fun out of it if your parents say those words! It's possible that your teen will take to deleting all his texts to stop your prying. In that case you can say that you know that he texts and it makes you very suspicious when there are no texts. Is your teen hiding something?

Again, not all kids *want* to talk dirty and send provocative pictures, like that 12-year-old boy. Let them know that if they're getting hassled by other kids to respond to sexy texts, they can say something like, "My stupid parents check my phone every day, and both of us will get in trouble, so don't send them anymore." This lets you take the blame and lets them off the hook. That's a good thing.

A cellphone, a computer, or any other device is a privilege, not an entitlement. As the grown-ups in the house, it's your job to make sure your teens are using them safely. You can't help if you don't know!

53 dealing with your teen's cellphone addiction

Here's the Problem

As a college instructor, I experience firsthand the consequences of cellphone addiction. In the old days before cellphones, I had my students' attention, except for the ones whose eyes had rolled up into their heads and were napping in class during a morning after the night before. Class discussions were lively, and participation was high. In my classes now, I see students with their hands on their laps, scrolling and texting away, too busy to participate in class discussions or take adequate notes. At the beginning of each new semester, when I ask my college students, "What will be your biggest challenge?" they all say, without reservation, staying away from their phones.

Cellphone distraction is one of the biggest issues I hear about from parents. "My teen never talks to me anymore. She just goes right up to her room and is on the phone for the rest of the day and night. My teen never talks to me in the car, preferring to be on the phone texting with friends. When we go to restaurants, my teen doesn't talk to us. He just gets on the phone and is either texting with friends or playing with his apps the whole time. It's so rude!"

A teen's phone addiction is fed during the day at school (where you thought your teen would spend six hours a day cellphone-free). Your teen uses the last 15 minutes of each class for thinking and planning what to text, post, Snapchat, or Instagram to whom as soon as class is dismissed! There are a lot of decisions to make! Missing 15 minutes of attention in class? No problem!

Finally, without realizing it, parents unwittingly feed into their teen's addiction. Think about how many times you've texted your teens during their day at school reminding them of their pickup time or whatever else feels time-sensitive. I know of many parents who end up getting into "texting arguments" with their teen during the day at school. Teens text to let parents know what they plan to do after school. Parents text back with a "NO WAY, you have too much homework. You come right home after school!" The teen is mad and spends her class time thinking about the next text she will send to her mom to convince her to change her mind.

The best way to deal with cellphone addiction is to prevent it from happening in the first place.

Why It's a Problem

Your teen has the keys to the candy store. If you were a teen and were faced with having to choose between talking to parents at the dinner table or carrying on with friends, or between sitting in silence in the car or texting with friends, or between listening to your teacher drone on and thinking about how you could make your friends laugh, or between studying algebra and texting with a girl you think is hot, which would you choose?

The emotional center of a teen's brain, which is more activated than the thinking part of the brain, is desperate for excitement. After all, candy is much more fun to eat than broccoli!

That's your teen's excuse. And here's yours: When you were a teenager, I'm guessing you did a little drinking, maybe a few drugs, and were definitely having some sex. These life experiences provide a roadmap for dealing with sex, drugs, and booze with your teens. But you didn't know the allure of cellphones in your youth, so you have no experience to draw on when it comes to your teen's use. Since you experienced the technology explosion as an adult, you expect that your teens will use technology like you do and that they'll have the same kind of discipline and manners as you. So you gave them their cellphones, happy that you had an immediate means of communication with them, never dreaming that this piece of plastic would completely take over their lives.

When parents make themselves available to their teens during the school day through texts, it feeds their addiction and interferes with their ability to delay gratification. They want an answer, and they want it NOW! Problem is, life isn't like that, and it's a disservice to your teens to let them think it is.

Here's the Solution

There really is no magic here. It's all about setting limits from the very beginning. But it's never too late to start. Here are some tips to keep the addiction from developing in the first place or to prevent it from getting worse.

→ For younger teens ages 10 to 13, limit daily cellphone use to 30 minutes after school and 30 minutes at night. Teens that age truly have nothing important to discuss, but if they have the option of using their phone, they will use it. Take away that option.

→ For teens 13 and up, have a protected two-hour period every day where there's no cellphone use. This should happen even if they don't have homework, and even during vacations and summers. Note: For non-smartphones, you can call your phone carrier and schedule shut-off and turn-on times like a DVR, so you can avoid the "I just need five more minutes" argument that will surely occur. For teens who already have smartphones, you can say, "Here are the times we've agreed on for taking a break from your phone. I don't want to get into arguments with you every time I come in for your phone. If you choose to argue, than I will choose to swap out your smartphone for a regular flip phone. Your choice."

→ Absolutely no smartphone (probably too late for a lot of you on this one).

→ No cellphones in bed during sleep time.

→ Don't text your child during the day at school; if it's time-sensitive, send a message through the office.

→ No cellphone use during family meals and outings.

→ Model good cellphone manners: Don't use your cellphone while you're driving your kids; don't text or check emails on your cellphone while with your kids in restaurants or at movies, sporting events, concerts, or plays.

This last tip is extremely important. Your teens watch your every move. If they see you constantly on your phone they will deduce that it's OK for them too. You are their most important role models. Use that positive power!

54 does my teen text too much?

if so what can I do about it?

Here's the Problem

The youth of today are getting better and faster in their ability to text at warp speed. Good for them! What an accomplishment. According to a Nielsen survey, in 2011 the average number of texts a teen sent a month was 2,280. In 2013 it's risen to an average of 3,339 per month. Broken down by gender, girls text 4,050 times per month, while boys are at 2,539 per month. Mind you, this is an average. Most parents tell me that every now and again they go to their online accounts just to take a peek at their kids' texting numbers and are shocked with the pages and pages tallying up to 10,000 to 15,000 a month. That's a lot of "whass-up?"

Texting for me and for many adults I know is a pain in the butt. I can't see the letters, I hate to misspell words but get too frustrated to correct them, and honestly I would rather speed-dial a number and say a few words. To me, texting is just too much work. But clearly to teens, it's easier—go figure. Wouldn't it be nice if the skills teens master with texting could be translated to writing term papers at warp speed? I'm thinking in the year 2025 term papers will be one long page full of "i thk hstry s fn."

Growing up with texting as their first line of communication has made teens completely mindless about when and where they text. My college students, lovely and sweet kids, sit in the front row of my classes and text away right in front of me. When I tap them on their shoulders with a "Really, right in front of me?" they blush and stammer, truly unaware of what they are doing!

Why It's a Problem

Connecting with friends is probably the single most important activity your teen does during the day. At least that's what your teen would say. When I was a teenager, my friendships were absolutely the most important part of my life, more than schoolwork, my parents, and chores. Friends always came first. I remember running to use my home phone (I'm old) to call my best friend even if I had just dropped her off five minutes before. We had a lot to talk about, gossiping and rehashing the previous afternoon or evening. When teens separate from parents and become more independent—an important phase of adolescence—friends become even more important. Teens are practicing the skills that will eventually lead them to healthy adult relationships. Cellphones provide them with *one* of the means to do that. They can reach their friends anytime and anywhere. Teens today never get a break from their friends and are rarely alone with their own thoughts. This is not a good thing. With no break from the chatter, teens have little time to do their own thinking and processing. Constant feedback from the world, and too little quiet time, inhibit a teen from developing a sense of self. In addition, teens are less comfortable with being alone with their thoughts. Again, this is not a good thing. We all need time to calm our brains and to concentrate on other things that may need our attention. For teens, that probably would be schoolwork!

Here's the Solution

You need to help your kids develop an awareness of how much they are texting. If you asked your teen to estimate how much time he spends texting a day, he would probably say, "Oh, a few hours." Believe me, it's way more than a few hours! Since most teens do not have to pay for their phones, it all feels free, both in terms of money and of responsibility. We have exempted them from feeling a sense of ownership for their behavior and for what it means to have this phone. A solution to this problem would be to include them in the process of bill paying. You continue to pay the bill, but in order to have the *privilege* of using the phone your teen would be required to actually look at a phone bill once a month. Make a monthly date together to go online to your account at your phone carrier's website. Have your teen look at the monthly cost of text messaging in black and white. Many kids will be shocked to see the amount of time this fills up. Helping them to understand the balance of work and play is an important prerequisite for being successful in life.

They may roll their eyes or give you attitude and think the whole thing is stupid. That's OK. You can say, "I get it. I know you think this is stupid, but I need you to see in print how you're using your phone. If you were mindlessly eating bags and bags of chips and wondering why you were gaining weight, I would hold up the empty bags of chips to show you. It's kind of the same thing."

Remember you're paying for the phone, and that does give you some rights. This should be nonnegotiable. It's texting use now, but in a few years it could be a credit card. This is about teaching responsibility and mindfulness. I have seen parents obsessively concerned with making sure their kids don't eat junk food or watch junk TV, but who let kids binge on their texting!

55 driving distracted
don't let their fingers do the talking when they're driving

Here's the Problem

You don't need a law to tell you that texting while driving is hazardous to your health. But some people need a little push, and knowing that Big Brother is watching, ready to hand out a ticket and a fine, may be the motivation they need to stow away the phone. Here's a scary statistic from the U.S. Centers for Disease Control and Prevention: 63 percent of people under 30 years old acknowledge driving while using a handheld phone, and 30 percent of people under 30 text while driving. In 2012, 5,500 people were killed in texting-and-driving accidents.

Why It's a Problem

Unfortunately, since teens lead with their hearts and not their brains, their worry about missing some really, really, really important tidbit of news overrides any worry about Big Brother or, more important, deadly car accidents. In fact, there's even a label for this addiction: FOMO, or "Fear of Missing Out." To counter this, most parents lead with parental lecture #92: Texting and talking on your phone while driving is verboten and will be met with severe consequences.

For some reason, when I hear the chime on my phone signifying a text, I get a little excited. Who is it? What do they want? Even though 99.99999 percent of the time it's nothing, somewhere I must think that the information just relayed is somehow going to change my life and that I can't live without knowing it immediately! Come on, admit it, you get that little surge of excitement too. Well that's what your teen is feeling, times 1,000. As an adult, I get that it is ridiculous, so I've trained myself not to look at the text until I have parked the car. I do have some ability to delay gratification. Most teens don't. Their whole world is now designed to feed this beast. Want to watch a movie? Instant download. Want to talk to a friend? Instant text. Want to make someone laugh? Instant photo!

In the heat of the moment, when kids get into that car, lecture #92 is nowhere present in their immediate consciousness. It's gone in one ear and out the other, unless it's been paired with a concrete action plan. And this, parents, is the key. Your teen's cellphone is practically an extension of her body. She's so used to feeling the weight of it in the palm of her hand that it doesn't register in her brain as an encumbrance. Teens have learned to navigate their world almost single-handedly (while the other hand texts). Your job is not just to lecture about the dangers of driving and cellphone use, but also to help develop a game plan for how to eliminate cellphone temptation while driving.

Recently I asked my 60 text-crazy college students how many of them text while driving. A depressingly large majority raised their hands. Then I asked them to visualize where their phones were when they got into the driver's seat. Here was the astounding response: They didn't know! That's because they don't think of their phones as being a separate part of their body. To them it's like asking where's your hand when you walk to the car? When I asked, "How about in your hand?" they laughed at the joke but got the message. Then I asked them to visualize where the phone was while they were driving. The two most popular answers were in their right hand or in their lap. Then we began to work on a plan. Clearly, they all got that the phone needed to be inaccessible to them while driving. The girls figured that if they put them in their bags—making sure the phone was on silent—and put their bags in the backseat, that would solve the problem. Out of sight, out of mind. The boys thought putting them on silent and in the glove compartment would do the trick. The learning is not someone telling them the obvious, but in helping them to develop a plan to change the behavior.

Here's the Solution

Don't wait for your teens to get their driver's licenses to put a plan in place. Integrating new behavior takes time. You'll need to start this process of helping your teen to be comfortable in the car without access to a cellphone. Trust me, this will take some time! I suggest at least six months to a year before obtaining the coveted license. You may get some resistance, but most teens are highly motivated to drive. They will acquiesce when they understand that in order to drive they'll need to be deemed cellphone-safe.

When your teen is a passenger in the front seat, there's no phone use at all. Have her develop a plan for what she'll do with her phone when she gets in the car. This will be hard. Teens will forget. They'll need their parents to remind them, every single time. It's important to be consistent in reminding them and to have realistic expectations. Remember, changing behavior is really, really hard. In this practice you are helping your teen to associate sitting in the front seat with no phone use, which will hopefully translate to no use in the driver's seat. This is classical conditioning. To help enforce this—because of course you will get tremendous opposition—use this "I get it" moment: "I get how important staying in touch with your friends is, but soon you'll be driving and I need to know that you're able to put away your phone and sit it out without talking or texting while driving. Having you do that with us while *we're* driving is a way of practicing and developing the ability to give your full attention to the road. This is obviously your choice. I'm not going to make you put your phone away, though I'll be happy to remind you. But when it comes time for you to get your license, I will probably not let you drive my car unless I have complete confidence that you can be in the car without being on your phone. I'll only know that because you'll have shown me. I love you, and your safety is always going to be the most important thing in the world to me!"

Once again, most important is what *you* do in the car with *your* phone. The model you set is the most powerful, more powerful than the lecture and more powerful than the plan. Your teens are watching your every move. If you talk or text on your phone while you're driving with them, just know that it will come back to bite you. You're likely to hear, "You talk on the phone while you're driving; what's the difference?" And truly there really is no answer to that. There's no correlation between driving experience and accidents with cellphone use. In fact, recent research shows that adults actually text while driving more than teens do. Twenty years as a driver, 20 days as a driver, distraction is distraction, and your kids will see the hypocrisy if that's your argument. So when your kids, and this includes young kids or teens, are in the car while you're driving, make sure you say out loud, "Shut my phone off for me. I don't want to be talking and driving." I want your kids to hear the words, so they get parked away up in those brains of theirs, so that when *they* get in that driver's seat, they have a tape playing in their heads from the most important people in their lives.

Practice makes perfect!

56

teens losing sleep
goodnight moon,
goodnight texting

Here's the Problem

If I've told you once, I've told you a million times, no texting after bedtime! A recent article in the *Boston Globe* interviewed a number of teens to understand the motivation behind bedtime texting. Here are a few quotes from this article. Read 'em and weep: "When I'm texting someone I don't feel alone." "When you don't have your phone, you feel incomplete." "It's impolite not to respond if someone is coming to you with their problems." One teen interviewed said that she gets as many as 100 texts while she's in bed. "I just don't feel like myself if I don't have my phone near me or I'm not on it."

Why It's a Problem

We've created texting-crazed monsters who are moving into adulthood terrified to be alone. This is not a healthy thing, either psychologically or physically. Adulthood requires us to have confidence in our ability to deal with complex emotions: depression, anxiety, loneliness, and stress. These are all the things that challenge us as we deal with career, family, and transitions of life. Adolescence is a training ground for developing coping mechanisms for managing all of this. Of course, reaching out to friends is an important strategy. Learning how to develop strong support systems is the main event of teen life. But it's equally important to know that we can also depend on ourselves in looking for a safe harbor. Look no further than a sleeping baby who sucks her thumb and hugs her teddy bear on her way to slumber.

Here's an example reported to me by a mom. Her 15-year-old boy is everyone's best friend. He's supportive, loving, and a great listener. He keeps his cellphone under his pillow on vibrate, just in case a friend needs him. At 2:30 a.m. his phone vibrates. Always on alert, he receives an SOS text from a girlfriend. She's just had a major blowup with her boyfriend and needs his help to sort it all out. Can he meet her at the local park? Remember it's 2:30 a.m. He agrees. His parents are tucked away in their room, none the wiser that their wonderful son has slipped out the back door. Walking the streets of his suburban neighborhood, he doesn't think much about safety or that the local police might be on their rounds patrolling. They were, and since he looked suspicious, they picked him up. His parents hear a knock on their door at 3:00 a.m. and are shocked to see their son standing between two cops. There goes a good night's sleep!

Physically speaking, this is a no-brainer. Teens are just not getting enough sleep. Experts on child and teen sleep have said that kids who text late into the night do not fall asleep as well, and they don't enter the deep sleep of stage 4 REM sleep. This is the time during sleep when the lessons of the day are stored away for retrieval from short-term memory to long-term memory. You know, all that important stuff they learn in school that they will be tested on! So forget about academic tutors and SAT tutors; it is all a waste of money unless you can get your teen to sleep!

When I speak to parents about this issue and tell them no cellphones in bed, the floodgates open with excuses such as "But he uses his phone as an alarm clock" or "I'll never be able to get her phone away from her." Hello! Buy them alarm clocks. And who is in charge here?

Here's the Solution

Getting your teen to accept that sleeping and cellphone use do not go together like two peas in a pod will be a challenge. Do a little homework first and look at your teen's phone bill. See if he's texting at night. If so, you have your ammunition. If not, you're ahead of the game, but it *will* happen. If you go into battle mode about this, you'll make a difficult situation worse. Don't approach your teen with "I'm taking your phone away at bedtime!

You're not sleeping! It's my phone, get over it!" This will not engender cooperation. Instead use this "I get it" moment: "I get how important it is for you
to have your phone with you in bed. I know you always like to be a thumb
away from all your friends in case they need you, or if something is going
on that is a 'must know.' But here's the thing: you need to sleep, you need
to give your brain a rest, and you need to learn to develop confidence in
your ability to get yourself to sleep. I know this will be an adjustment, but
I have complete confidence in you." Expect resistance, anger, and hostility.
It will not be pretty. No need to get defensive; just give a little shoulder
shrug and you're done.

For those teens with non-smartphones, cellphone companies now have a
service for a few extra bucks a month that will disable the outgoing and
incoming calls and texts for a specific period of time, for example, 11 p.m.
to 6 a.m. I recommend this approach rather than physically taking the phone
away so as to avoid a "please just a few more minutes!" power struggle. For
those of you who have given your teens smartphones, you can't disable the
phone. You'll have to get your teens to turn them over. Let them know that
the choice is theirs. Either hand you the phone at a mutually agreed-upon
time, or you will switch out the smartphone for a flip phone that you can
have shut off in magic phone land. And if your teen says, "But my phone is
an alarm clock," get your teen an alarm clock!

Stand firm on this one. It is a matter of health!

57 should I buy my teen a smartphone?

Here's the Problem

I feel like an old fart! During coaching sessions with parents and at my parenting seminars, I am frequently asked whether parents should buy their teen a smartphone. As I answer, I hear my mother's voice in my head: "Why does a 16-year-old need a fancy phone like that?" Teens do not need fancy phones that provide unlimited access to the Internet and unlimited social networking sites like Facebook, Twitter, Tumblr, Instagram, Kik, Snapchat, and SnapVideo, to name a few. Parents may go to the trouble of blocking some of these sites from their teens' laptops and home computers to limit distraction, but that's an ineffective strategy when the teens have these same applications on their smartphones, which are never out of sight or hand!

Why It's a Problem

When teens have personal entertainment and communication systems in their hot little hands 24/7, there's no need to hang with the family. Perhaps you have placed your home computer in a public space like the kitchen or family room to encourage interaction and supervision of your teens during homework and computer time. But these activities account for the smallest percentage of your teens' time after school and on weekends, maybe only an hour or two. That still leaves many hours a day for your teens to engage in unsupervised, distracting, and unhealthy activities. With their smartphones they can download and watch their favorite TV shows or movies, download unsafe and questionable Internet content such as porn or weird social networking sites, and spend hours keeping up with the multiple social networking sites that require attention and posting, not all of which are safe. If they're busy doing all these addictive activities, they're not spending as much time doing homework or with the family. When teens have smartphones, these very important competing interests are often the first to go. If your teen wasn't distracted enough with texting, just think of all the hours he can waste with his new "toy."

Something unique is also at play here: Parents and teens have simultaneously "jumped into the pool." Parents may have purchased their teen's smartphone on the same day as they bought one for themselves. How cool to be able to share in the fun together. Because, make no mistake about it, smartphones are fun! For adults, having all this technology is useful in the workplace and at home. Smartphones give you the ability to organize and optimize busy lives and, yes, have fun as well. Adults have the experience to know when enough is enough. They can shut off and rejoin families, friends, and colleagues for that face-to-face time. But teens lack that experience. They do not have the discipline or perspective to realize that spending hours upon hours on phones can be detrimental. What starts out as a wonderful gift, and a moment of gratitude from your teen, ends up with arguments galore. *"If you don't put away that damn phone and do your homework, I will take it away!"* You are now faced with the daily power struggle of pulling your teen away from a favorite toy. And the sad part is that it was totally avoidable.

Here's the Solution

This will seem so obvious. Don't buy your teen a smartphone. Your teen will be angry and think you are the meanest parent alive. You absolutely will hear, "Everybody else has one!" In truth, many kids do. You can say, "I get that this decision is hard. I get that seeing all your friends have something you really want can make you feel like a loser. The good news is you still have a phone, you can still text your friends, and you can still use the computer to share in the fun of Twitter and Facebook. You just won't be able to have access to it every minute of every day. We're OK being the bad guys here, knowing that we are helping you to become the best person you can be. So if you want to be mad at us, that's OK, we can handle it."

58 a scary story
the misuse of smartphones

Here's the Problem

The curse and the gift of a smartphone is that it can do so many things and function in so many ways. The video camera that lives in a smartphone is fantastic for capturing a spontaneous memorable moment that otherwise would have been lost. In the hands of a responsible person who understands the boundaries of privacy and what's appropriate to share, having access to video making is a gift. If you're an impulsive teen who lacks the maturity and judgment needed to protect other people from humiliation, a smartphone can be a curse.

Why It's a Problem

A dad shared this story with me. He was beside himself—ashamed for his child and angry with himself for buying into the hype of "everybody else has a smartphone" when his teen asked for one. After all, it seemed de rigueur for the well-connected teen.

A high school student was sitting in one of his classes. The teacher was apparently new and a bit green, and often lost control of her class. Because of this, the inmates were running the prison, if you know what I mean. This student decided to use his smartphone to secretly record the teacher as she tried in vain to get her students to pay attention. After he shared the video with a couple of friends, it spread like wildfire, eventually landing on Facebook, where the entire high school could see it.

You can imagine the humiliation this teacher suffered. Committing to the teaching profession, with low pay and little job security, is not an easy decision these days. Young people who go into teaching do it for the love of the profession and the desire to do good. How upsetting it must have been for this teacher to be so betrayed and disrespected by her students.

Having said that, I understand the student's motivation. Clearly there had been discussion among the students about this teacher. In the old days, students would have just talked behind her back. Maybe the students would have told their parents. And maybe the parents would have voiced their concern to the principal, who then might have provided the teacher with more supervision and mentoring. Problem addressed, check! Now that kids have video cameras on their phones and their phones are with them in the classroom, what fun to actually have a permanent record of this teacher's performance.

When the video was posted on Facebook and seen by a parent monitoring (thank God) her teen's Facebook, it was brought to the attention of the principal. It turns out that it's against the law to make an audio recording of somebody without his or her permission. The police were called, and they were able to deduce the origin of the video (which, since it had sound, was illegally made). This fun prank has now become a criminal offense! Who knew? The student who took the video and the student who posted it were both read their rights and arrested!

This is serious stuff. Of course, the kids involved had no idea. To them, it was just a prank. It was fun. It felt powerful. After all, other kids will think it's funny that this teacher didn't "catch" this student filming her.

Needless to say, if the student didn't have a smartphone in the first place, this incident would never have happened.

This is not a story about a group of bad kids. It's a story about teenagers, who, in general, lack impulse control, get caught up in the possibility of "awesomeness," and are given too much technology without the training and understanding of the responsibility that goes with it. That's on us, the adults.

Here's the Solution

Kids do stupid things without thinking. As adults we shouldn't set them up to fail by giving them things like fancy technology that they're developmentally unable to manage. We have to understand that a teen's decision-making capacity is not at its best . . . yet. It's not about trust; it's about temptation.

The obvious fix to this potential problem is not to give your teen a smartphone. But I accept that many parents do. If this is your case, tell your teen this story. Make sure she understands the law. Make sure she knows that if she makes a video without the permission of the subjects and chooses to publicly post the video, she may be leaving herself open to criminal charges. Parents, help your teens to understand that when videos are posted and shared, they can be viewed by the unexpected: parents, principals, coaches, prospective college admissions officers, potential employers, and teachers. Any one of these responsible parties will be sure to track down the "director" if they feel someone's rights have been violated or if the behavior on the video is dangerous or doesn't meet with the expectations of what's reasonable behavior. You might say to your teen, "I get that teens love to video their friends doing stupid and funny things, but you'll need to decide if posting that video to get some short-term attention is worth jail time or being denied the job or college you really want!"

teaching your teen safe posting
the too-much-information dilemma

Here's the Problem

Curiosity about "what kind of stuff my kid is posting these days" motivated a mom to check out her daughter's Facebook wall. The mom called me after reading a post that began, "You'll never guess what my mom said the other day about my brother." Her daughter went on to describe one of those private, good-natured teasing moments when you make a little fun, in a loving way, at a family member's character trait. What this mom read on her daughter's Facebook wall was a detailed recitation of this family's teasing moment directed at her 11-year-old son. These are not moments a family wants outed for public consumption lest they be misinterpreted. In a private family moment, the boy was fine with the teasing, but when it was shared as entertainment for his sister's hundreds of Facebook friends, absolutely not! It was embarrassing to the boy and mortifying for the mom. Needless to say, Mom was furious. "How could she be so stupid? Doesn't she know how it will make her brother feel? Our family is private! How can I ever trust her again?"

It used to be that Facebook and texting were the preferred vehicles for posting these kinds of anecdotes. Now there are myriad social networking sites and applications to choose from. Twitter allows teens to transmit information at lightning speed to hundreds more people than just their "friends" on Facebook. Remember all it takes is one retweet and the audience has grown exponentially. Using Twitter is an excellent way of notifying many people simultaneously of party locations, hang locations, and secret rendezvous spots. A parent told me about her son and his friends who saw that a house in their town, with an in-ground swimming pool, seemed to be devoid of occupants. After some reconnaissance work the teens determined that the family was away for a vacation. In a tweeting instant, literally hundreds of teens showed up for the "most awesome drinking and pool party ever"—read unsafe.

Perhaps it's a Saturday night and you and your honey decide to have a date night. The only one in your house without definite plans is your teen. You leave the house confident that he's snug as a bug in a rug and in for the night. Oh, he's in for the night all right, along with 30 or 40 of his closest friends, who stop by the moment you step out! All it took were seven simple words posted on Facebook or Twitter: "So bored, parents out, nothing to do." And the rest is history.

Why It's a Problem

When teens post on Facebook or Twitter or Instagram, they think, "How cool can I be? How funny can I be? How outrageous can I be?" Teens are smack in the middle of developing a personal identity. To do that, they need to try on different personas to see what fits. Sometimes their nature gets in the way. Perhaps they're shy and want to experiment with being someone else, so they develop an alter ego: "*I can't be this funny or brave or outrageous in person, but I can be on Facebook and Twitter.*" The teen girl who posted the story about her brother wasn't thinking beyond "This is funny, and everyone will think *I'm* funny!"

Teen brains have difficulty thinking things through to possible consequences. Were a teen to use sequential thinking it might look like this: "If I post this story about my brother, and my friends read it, then they might think it's all right to tease my brother and make him feel bad. And this does make my mom look a little insensitive. I know she was only kidding, but other people might not. I think I won't post this on my Facebook wall." Wouldn't it be a beautiful thing if kids went through this kind of thinking before they said or did something that seems crazy to us frontal-cortex-thinking adults? But alas, teens are spontaneous and impulsive, not thoughtful and careful.

Here's the Solution

Expecting that teens will instinctively know how to navigate the real world is unrealistic. Unfortunately, Internet use is based on instant gratification, which is the energy force of adolescence. Giving your teens a framework of what may and may not be posted is a must. They need help in understanding the consequences of their behavior and strategies that give them better control of those impulsive thoughts.

Here is how the mom in that first example might talk to her daughter: "I get that it's fun to post things on Facebook that are outrageous and funny. You should feel free to do that. But it is not OK to post things about our family or friends or people you might know that could be embarrassing or hurt their feelings. You also can't post things that give out too much personal information, like our address or your phone number, or our family's plans for weekends and vacations. I know you weren't thinking this when you posted that story about your brother. But if one of your friends were to say something to your brother after reading this, he would be devastated. I know how much you love your brother and I know you would never knowingly do something to hurt him. So here's a new rule: No writing about our family without permission. You and I together will check your public postings on Twitter and Facebook at the end of every day for the first few weeks to make sure there's nothing on there that could potentially be hurtful or gives out too much personal information. If your postings seem OK, then we will check in on them every few weeks. I get that this is a learning process."

Education + Consequence = Change

a "friending" intervention

teaching your teen how to "make friends" on social networking sites

Here's the Problem

Do you think the dictionary has "friending" in its newest edition? The spell check on my computer keeps telling me that it's not a word. Oh, it's a word all right! I have a paltry 147 "friends" on Facebook and I am proud to say I know every one of them.

Your teen, on the other hand, probably has well over 500, of whom 400 are total strangers. But the guys are probably "hot" and the girls "hotter," and therefore they fit the criteria for "friending."

As adults we're well aware of the dangers of these anonymous friends. Just pick up any newspaper any day of the week and read the sad story of a young girl who "fell in love" with someone on Facebook, only to find him to be a creepy adult male predator. In fact, there's a show on MTV called *Catfish* that documents a new story like this every week. Watch it with your teen; it's an eye-opener.

Facebook is not the only site for teens to socialize with potential strangers. New social networking applications are sprouting up like flowers in the spring, thanks to smartphones. Kik is a messaging application that many teens are fond of. Why? Because most parents don't know about it, and teens feel freer to "express" themselves away from the prying eyes of their parents, who are often their "friends" on Facebook. This is a very unsafe app.

When partnered with Instagram, teens can be introduced to people world-wide in an instant, and most of them are not teens!

Here's how it works: Teens with Instagram accounts can post their Kik usernames in their Instagram profiles. Perhaps they were tagged in a photo that a friend posted, and perhaps that photo was reposted multiple times by multiple people. Somewhere in that chain, a person might think your son or daughter is cute and want to connect with him or her. All they need to do is go to your son's or daughter's Instagram profile, get the Kik username, and connect directly. *Voila!* A new "friend" is made. And this friend happens to be a stranger.

Why It's a Problem

Teenagers are like "junkies" when it comes to wanting and getting attention. Their adolescent brains are hardwired for that. The self-consciousness that is so much a part of teen life comes from a new understanding that other people think things about them. This is a big change from childhood, when kids define themselves by how they measure up: "I'm the tallest in my class. I'm the slowest runner in my gym class." As a teen there is a new level of thinking: "I'm the slowest runner in my gym class, AND everyone thinks I'm a fat loser!" Sometimes the attention is unwanted, but most of the time it's coveted. "Look how many 'friends' I have. Everyone thinks I'm cool and hot and funny!" You can see how addictive it can become. Facebook, Twitter, Instagram, and Kik are attention-delivery systems! But because the "understanding consequences" part of the brain is overruled with excitement and attention, teens do not pay attention to the dangers of connecting with a stranger.

Here's the Solution

Lecturing on this topic is an inferior tool. Teens think they are smarter than adults and will either stop listening or argue that this could never happen to them. That's teen magical thinking for you. One strategy is to periodically ask your teen to go through his "friends" on Facebook, Twitter, and Instagram with you, explaining his connection with each friend. Your teen might not like your nosiness no matter how teen-friendly you make the conversation. "You know honey, I get how much fun it is when someone new 'friends' you on Facebook or seeks you out on Twitter or Instagram. There are people out there that hope and pray that they can find young teens gullible enough to swallow any story they may give you about themselves. Additionally, they prowl these sites for information that most teens post about really personal stuff, and who knows how they will use it. What do you do to screen requests from new people?" Cue teen eye rolling! No matter, it's worth a try. At the least it will send a clear message about safety. Make sure that you help your teen develop some way to screen for weirdos. Remember, just saying "Don't do that" is not a strategy!

As an alternative, I have a dual-purpose, out-of-the-box strategy. It gives you firsthand information about your teen's "friending" criteria, as well as forgoing the "talk." This is an "actions speak louder than words" approach. Create a new Facebook page and profile under a new name and appropriate gender. If you have a daughter, be a guy, and if you have a son, be a girl. Upload a photo to your new profile of a hot guy or girl as appropriate. Make a "friend request" to your son or daughter.

Here comes the learning piece. If your son or daughter does in fact "friend" you, there's definitely something to talk about! Don't start by saying how stupid your teen was to "friend" a stranger. This will not be a good conversation starter. What you can say is, "Honey, I did this little experiment to show you how easily you 'friend' someone that you don't know. I know it's flattering to get attention, but let's come up with a strategy to help you weed out the people that are OK and the people that aren't. I love you and just want you to be safe. Just so you know I have deleted this fictitious person, never to bother you again." This method really does teach a valuable lesson. Actions *always* speak louder than words!

The bottom line is that no teen needs access to all these different social networking sites. One or two should suffice. Kik should never be an app on your teen's phone or computer. Make sure you are the *only* person authorized to download applications on your teen's smartphone, especially the free ones. You may need to go to your local phone store for training on your teen's phone.

Remember, you're the gatekeeper for your teen's safety.

61 to give or not to give
my parents, my passwords

Here's the Problem

A parent at one of my seminars asked me what she should do about her 16-year-old son who refused to share his Facebook password. The teen cited privacy as his rationale. I've also had reports from many parents that their teens rebuff parental requests for smartphone passwords, saying, "It's my phone, and it's none of your business!" When parents back down on these requests, it leaves them with no means to monitor what their teens are posting on social networking sites and with whom they're sharing information. Also for teens with smartphones, parents have no control over the kinds of apps their teens download and how these apps are being used. It's an issue of safety and of supervision.

Why It's a Problem

When parents ask for something from their teen and their teen refuses, it sets up a power struggle that leaves parents looking ineffectual and powerless. This is a problem because it sets up an unhealthy dynamic between parents and teenagers where teens feel stronger and more in control than their parents. Not good, and not safe! The truth is that parenting a teen is very different from parenting a younger child. Developmentally speaking, younger children love rules. They love knowing them, making them, and following them.

Teens, on the other hand, hate rules! One of the major themes of adolescence is power and control. They are driven to fight for control over their own lives, preparing them for adulthood. During the teen years, it's extremely important for parents to avoid power struggles and give choices rather than ultimatums.

The other obvious problem with relinquishing authority to your teen regarding password sharing is safety. The impulsiveness of teen behavior leaves them open to poor decision making. All that texting and tweeting, photo and video sharing, and making new "friends" leaves teens vulnerable to mishaps and even danger. They need help in this area, even though they would vehemently disagree! Teens lack life experience, and they're still working on developing the ability to think things through to their logical consequences. There will come a time, around age 17 or 18, when your teens *will be* responsible for their own decisions, their behavior, and the consequences. Hopefully, the supervision and education you've provided up until that point will positively impact this new stage of independence.

Here's the Solution

It's pretty simple, really. Parents absolutely need access to their teens' passwords. This is nonnegotiable. It should be part of any agreement you make with your teens when you give them the "privilege" of having laptops, smartphones, and iPads. If your teen chooses to refuse access, don't back down and don't go into battle mode. Neither is very effective. Instead, give your teen choices:

→ In the case of the Facebook password refusenik, you might say, "You have a choice. You can share your password with us so that we can make sure that you are safely using Facebook, or you can choose to have your computer access limited to common spaces in our house. This means there will be no bedroom use of the laptop at all. Your choice!"

→ For teens who have refused to share smartphone or smartpad passwords, they too have a choice. It might go like this: "I get how important your phone/pad is to you. I know there are a ton of fun things you can do on it and fun ways of connecting with your friends. We want to make sure that you are the best person you can be, and we'll need to make sure that there isn't too much of any-thing—apps, downloaded TV shows, movies, games—going on your device. We will also want to make sure that any photos or videos you might have are OK. If you choose to share your password, you can continue to have a smartphone/pad, and together we'll check it periodically. If you choose to withhold the password, then you're choosing to switch out your smartphone for a non-smartphone and give up your iPad. Your choice!"

These are hard decisions for parents. It's a new century, full of exciting new technology that we want our children to experience and be a part of. But unfortunately, there's no roadmap. Today's parents are pioneers, experiencing and learning about this new frontier of technology along *with* their kids, not ahead of them, as in previous generations. Teens may act as if they know more than their parents when it comes to technology, and it's true about the technical aspects. But when it comes to knowing what's best for them in the long run, you know best!

62 facebook + alcohol posts = problem drinkers

Here's the Problem

Research from a 2011 study published in the *Archives of Pediatric and Adolescent Medicine* found that kids who posted photos on Facebook of themselves deep into "partying mode" or who commented on how "trashed" they were were four times as likely to be problem drinkers compared with other kids who didn't comment on their alcohol or drug use on the site.

One positive outcome of monitoring your teen's social networking sites, especially Facebook, Twitter, and Instagram, is that you get a "fly on the wall" perspective of your teen's interactions with friends. These postings are a valuable opportunity to get a handle on your teen's emotional well-being. When you see your teen posting regularly about "partying," as in the study above, or about anger at the world, like one of the Boston Marathon bombers, or maybe about feelings of sadness and hopelessness, you should know that these are red flags.

Why It's a Problem

Teens who start drinking heavily in high school have a much higher likelihood of abusing alcohol and drugs as an adult. Perhaps your teen has been a savvy drinker and has developed good alcohol-masking techniques. Maybe you're asleep when he comes in at night so you never actually see him drunk. Maybe she covers her alcohol breath with mints and gum to avoid detection. Maybe there are regular weekend sleepovers at a friend's house where there is little parental supervision and the kids can get drunk with complete abandon. If this is the case, Facebook, Twitter, or Instagram may be your only window into your teen's "outside" life. It's important for parents to recognize the difference between casual drug or alcohol use and problem drinking or drug abuse so that intervention can begin as early as possible. Your teen may be having problems with alcohol and drugs, excessive anger, or depression. Undetected, these problems can grow into a scary and dangerous future. If you don't know, you can't help.

Here's the Solution

Monitor your teen's Facebook, Twitter, and Instagram postings. Rather than just paying attention to the language they use, like the profanity and the sexually provocative, observe the subtext. This means going past the "gross out" and getting to the gut. Is your teen posting regularly about his partying "prowess" or sexual conquests? Does he talk too much about hating this world and the people in it? If so, it's time for a conversation: "I recently checked out your Facebook posts and noticed that you talk a lot about partying (or hating the world). That really worries me. I get that kids like to party and talk about it, but your posting goes way past that. You talk about it much more than any of your friends. This recent study has found a relationship between posting and problems."

Your teen will not like this conversation. He will deny, minimize, and be furious with you. You have to work really hard not to get defensive. The issue is *not* that he posted this on Facebook. The issue is that you are worried about his safety. You must separate these two very, very different issues. The first issue requires you to provide consequences for inappropriate posting. The second requires you to seek treatment for your teen.

icky new social networking sites . . . beware!

Here's the Problem

Keeping up with new social networking sites can be a full-time job. But keep up you must! Your teen's safety depends on it. Unlike Facebook, some of these new sites feature live video feeds. Applications such as Skype seem so innocent in comparison. How wonderful Skype is! It allows you to watch your grandchildren take their first steps. Now imagine girls at a sleepover at one house, and boys at another. Let your imagination run wild. In fact, think "Girls Gone Wild." Imagine sexualized dancing and striptease. Yes, these things *do* go on. At least on Skype you have to know the person you're calling. But on sites like Omegle.com, Chatroulette.com, and the newest offering, Airtime, you do not know the person(s) you are chatting with.

These sites not only have a tremendous "ick" factor, but they can be dangerous as well. These are sites and chat rooms that resemble regular online chat rooms but now use the added attraction of live video. So basically there's no screening involved. Anyone can click on the site and they are on stage, live and in person. A parent I know wanted to check one out after she heard her 12-year-old daughter talking about it. It was only seconds after the mom signed on when someone's video came up and said, "Hi, where are you?" She freaked out. All of a sudden there was this strange man in her room asking questions, and she signed off immediately. But then she is a responsible, thinking, sane adult, not a teen.

I heard about Chatroulette from a parent with a 19-year-old son who was home for college break. Walking into his room one evening to say good night, she found him having video sex with some naked strange girl. Mom left the room shocked, disgusted, nauseated, and scared.

Another particularly damaging site is Ask.fm. Teens can go there and set up a profile. Anyone can then go to this teen's profile and offer anonymous questions and comments about this person. Teens commenting on the profile do not have to reveal their identity. This site is notorious for cyberbullying. How fun to tell people exactly what you think about them without worrying that you can be identified.

Why It's a Problem

I'm sure that many of your teens already know about these sites, which spread like wildfire. All it takes is one kid who's heard about it to bring it up on her laptop while friends are over, and it's off to the races. I know that teens see this as a fun party game. *"Hey, let's go on Chatroulette and check out the guys!"* There's tons of nudity and titillating sexual behavior for their pleasure. Some teens—feeling socially awkward, needing attention, or just plain horny—may begin to access this site on a regular basis in lieu of actual human contact. This is psychologically unhealthy and could potentially put them in communication with people who will take advantage of them in the future. The parent who found her son having "sex" on this site subsequently discovered he was actually in something of a relationship with an underage girl. He was 19 and planning to visit her in the summer, halfway across the country, in a town where the term "shotgun wedding" means real shotguns. It was a huge worry that this young man could have been charged with statutory rape. Scary stuff.

Another smart parent remarked that once the image is online it can be reproduced, and there you have pornography in the making. We're not just talking about still shots here but actual video.

According to newspaper, magazine, and TV news reports, Ask.fm has been linked to a number of teen suicides. A parent writes in an Internet chat, "I'm really concerned about my daughter who already suffers with depression. She has no close friends and turned to this site as a way to make friends and chat with people, but the abuse she has received on there is sick and disgusting. She's been told to kill herself several times and her name has been sent to others by these bullies asking them to bully her and make her kill herself!"

It is almost unbelievable that teens would taunt someone this way. I wish I had an explanation that made sense. But the best I can come up with is that teens get caught up in a "crowd" mentality. If a teen has a grudge against someone and that someone is on Ask.fm, then getting friends to "help" you torture this person becomes a weird test of loyalty. And the "best" part is that nobody can get in trouble because it is anonymous.

You might wonder why a teen that's being bullied would stay on this site. A logical move would be to take your profile down. Why be a glutton for punishment? Teens report that they would rather know what people think about them. If kids are acting weird toward them at school, then at least they know why. How convoluted is this? If they didn't have an available profile, then people couldn't write about them! That's teen thinking for you.

Here's the Solution

Have I grossed you out enough? Think of this as a teaching moment. You might ask your teen, "Have you heard about these new sites, Chatroulette or Omegle? They sound so scary and dangerous to me. There's so much potential for teens to be taken advantage of by skanky people. If you know anybody who goes on these sites, you should warn them. I get how kids might be attracted to sites like this, but there are real sexual perverts who stalk these sites. They are good at tracking down people they find enticing. This is really dangerous and scary. There may be a time when you are with your friends, and everyone thinks it would be fun to go on one of these sites. If you can't convince them not to, or you just want to get away, you can always text me, and I will call the house and say there is a family emergency and I have to come and get you." Give teens a strategy to exit and save face, and then scare the hell out of them!

Find out if your teen is on Ask.fm. You will only know by going on that site and seeing whether he has posted a profile. If so, I strongly suggest you block it on his laptop and make sure it's a blocked app on his smartphone as well. There are a slew of other social networking sites to choose from, and there is absolutely no upside to this site.

As the parent of a teenager, it's important for you to stay as current as you can. You can't talk to your teen about sites you don't know about. Every month or so you should Google "most popular social networking sites + teens." Familiarize yourself with these sites, arm yourself with information, and get ready to go into battle!

64 facebook posts that could put your teen in jail

threats that are taken seriously

Here's the Problem

Newspapers are full of stories these days about teens using Facebook and other social networking sites as a public forum for everyone and everything they hate. How about this news headline: "Nevada Girls Arrested in Teacher Threat Case." It seems that six middle school kids, feeling negatively about their school experience (read with sarcasm), invited their fellow students on Facebook to take part in "attack a teacher day." The challenge was to post as many crazy ways as they could think of to hurt or injure their teachers during the school day. The students took on this challenge with relish. An astute parent, supervising his teen's Facebook wall, was shocked at the viciousness of the threats and called the school and the police. The six ringleaders said they were only fooling around. But I'm guessing the targeted teachers didn't think it was funny.

Thank goodness an attentive parent found this conversation on his son's Facebook wall: "Let's commit a mass homicide. We'll use gallons of gasoline and thousands of syringes full of bear tranquilizers, and hey how about shooting some guns at children." Through their lawyer, the kids said they were only kidding. I guess they aren't laughing now. They were arrested and expelled from school.

And finally this story: Two teen boys were arrested after posting what seemed like a credible rant about going to the local high school, killing the school cop and front desk people, and doing a "Columbine all over again." Luckily, a Facebook "friend" saw these posts and notified his counselor at the high school. The boys were promptly arrested and held on $10,000 cash bail. If they are found guilty they can face up to 20 years in prison and fines up to $50,000. Putting up a rant on Facebook is serious business!

Why It's a Problem

Teens love talking "trash" on Facebook. They use it as a performance space. Their imaginary "audience"—a term that describes a teen's perception that everyone is looking at them and judging them—drives this behavior and contributes to the motivation to be center stage. It's what drives much of the behavior that's on Facebook, other social networking sites, and their cellphones. Sometimes teens post crazy things just to get noticed. And other times teens read the outrageous comments their friends post and try to "out outrageous" them. The audience awaits their "performance." Parents of teens need to understand that this drive is powerful!

Here's the Solution

You can't lecture your teen out of this very normal part of adolescent development. You only need to think back to your own teenage years and the crazy things you did with your friends. But life in this century is scarier, and rants and raves on Facebook, other social networking sites, and cellphones are public. Teens posturing on the field behind the school with their friends is different than when it's on a computer for thousands of people to see. It might be taken at face value. Is it a real threat or a joke? That's the million-dollar question. Given the number of school shootings, suicides, and bullying over the past few years, it's no joke!

Here is the conversation you need to have with your teen: First tell her about these stories and the consequences for the kids who posted threats on Facebook "because it's fun." Then you can say, "I get that kids use Facebook to be outrageous, but they often forget that once something goes on that page it's in the public domain. Even if you were only 'fooling around,' someone else might not read it that way. If you see something on Facebook that crosses a line, I hope you tell someone. You can do it anonymously if you want. But any threat could be a real one. Knowing that you could have done something but didn't could give you a lot of guilt to live with. Posting something just because it sounds good without thinking it through can get you in a lot of trouble. Just ask these kids who are facing jail time. Here are some guidelines I think will help you in the thinking-through process."

Here are my four golden rules for using Facebook and all other social networking sites:

→ Will this post hurt someone's feelings?

→ Will this post feel threatening to anyone?

→ Does this post give too much information about myself?

→ Is there anything in this post that another person could read and misinterpret?

Go over them with your teen. Type them up and post them in the bedroom, or wherever your teen uses the phone or computer, as reminders of safe social networking. Tell your teen they are as important as the rules you have to learn before you can get your driver's license. When she rolls her eyes and takes down the rules, let her know that there will be no phone and no computer unless the rules stay up. This is an important strategy for bringing reality and mindfulness into your teen's life. Call it a subliminal technique. Accidental glances at these rules while mindlessly typing away on their phone and computer day after day are bound to find their way into that teenage brain.

I know kids will be kids. But between Columbine, Virginia Tech, Newtown, Aurora, and the Boston Marathon bombing, how do you know when someone is "just kidding"? I know Facebook is fun. I'm glad we have it. But as an adult, I am aware of the consequences. Unfortunately, most teens are too swept up in their moment of "fun" to take the time to answer those four simple questions.

Kids aren't by nature "meanies," but they feel the power of "the word." It's fun to shock. The trouble is that they don't have enough life experience to know that sometimes shock creates fear, and fear creates action. Parents: Please continue to educate your teens about social networking and its power, the good, the bad, and the creepy!

social networking and the stolen identity

keeping your teens safe from other teens

Here's the Problem

A parent called me because her daughter was getting blamed for bad-mouthing kids on Facebook. It turns out that her daughter had not signed up for Facebook. Someone else—a "friend" of this girl—had created a page "in her name." The friend thought it would be funny to set up a fake Facebook page using her friend's name and bad-mouth kids without having to take personal responsibility for it. Thank God the mom and dad were great detectives and doggedly pursued Facebook and local authorities to help them figure out who was responsible. But the damage was already done, and this poor kid was getting blamed for saying hurtful things she had not said. Middle school is hard enough. Contending with the school rumor mill was almost too much for this girl to bear.

Another mom writes about her daughter's experience with Ask.fm: "We have had a campaign of hate against our daughter because an account has been set up in her name and apparently linked to her Twitter account. (This means that whatever is said on Ask.fm automatically goes on her daughter's Twitter feed, reaching hundreds of people.) The bogus comments on Ask.fm were intended to insult and hurt kids at her school. Since it's in her name, her friends believe she's responsible for the comments, and now there's a campaign of hate against her. More than 30 of her fellow students surrounded her at school. Some of these kids told her to die, and that everyone hates her. How absolutely unfair and cruel!"

Why It's a Problem

This cautionary tale for parents underscores the need for constant supervision when it comes to teens and their use of social networking sites. Teens are using these sites in ways that parents never imagined. When today's parents were teens and wanted to get back at someone they believed had wronged them, they might have spread rumors or talked behind their back to their friends. Now teens have a multitude of options to "get back" or cause major trouble for anyone against whom they have a vendetta.

Betrayal is a major theme of adolescence. Relationships and intimacy are brand new. Because of this, they don't really get the work it takes to form honest and trusted friendships. Feelings get hurt. As younger children, their biggest worry was "who will play with me?" Very little thought goes into the dynamics of the relationship. Any warm body will do! In the teen years, relationships take on new meanings. Sharing secrets is an important element in these new friendships, which make them ripe for betrayal. Adding insult to injury, teens are particularly susceptible to drama of any kind, thanks to the amygdala, the emotional center of the brain, which is highly active during teen brain development. High emotion, impulsivity, and technology can be a recipe for disaster.

Here's the Solution

For parents, keeping up with teens and technology often feels like a continuous game of "whack-a-mole." Just when you think you have control of one site, a million more sites pop up. It's almost impossible to keep up. But keep up you must. For starters, find out which social networking sites your teen uses. This is baseline information. Explain that you need it for safety reasons. How can you anticipate situations they could be faced with if you don't know where they "hang out"? If your teen seems evasive, do your own search. Plug her name into Twitter, Instagram, Facebook, and Ask.fm. Has she posted her profile? If there is something there that doesn't jibe with what your teen has shared, that's where the conversation should start.

Share the two stories I related, and ask your teen if she has heard about this kind of thing happening to someone she knows. Let her know that you know what can happen when teens get mad at each other and want to find a fast way to get payback. Be careful not to be judgmental and critical when you broach this subject. You're looking for conversation here, not interrogation. Comments such as "I can't believe kids are so cruel to each other" will shut down the conversation.

It's also important to let your teen know during this conversation that if something like this should happen to her, the sooner you know the sooner you can help her deal with it. This avoids having to get the school or the police involved.

"Be prepared" should be the mantra of parents of teens. Staying ahead of the game, rather than just going from crisis to crisis, teaches teens an important life lesson.

I'll give you my password if you give me yours

going steady in the 21st century

Here's the Problem

Do you remember "going steady" for the first time? It's always been important to have a talisman that represents your commitment. Perhaps it was a ring, an ID bracelet, or a necklace. It was something tangible you could hold to your heart and kiss goodnight while thinking of your beloved. I guess that's old-fashioned now. Today, teens share their Facebook, email, and phone passwords as a sign of trust and commitment. Tiffany, a 17-year-old teen girl interviewed on this subject, said, "I have nothing to hide from him and he has nothing to hide from me. I know he'd never do anything to hurt my reputation."

Oh, the beautiful naiveté of adolescence! True love lasts forever, which for teens is a week from Monday, when there is a painful and emotional breakup because Tiffany or her beloved and trustworthy boyfriend flirted with someone else!

It turns out, according to Pew research, that 30 percent of teens share passwords with their girlfriends and boyfriends.

Why It's a Problem

Teens live in the present and do not practice thinking things through to their logical consequences. It's not that the teen brain is incapable of sequential thinking. It's that teen brains are dominated by impulses and emotions. For example, prior to sharing a password, it would be unlikely for a teen to wonder how a boyfriend or girlfriend would use a shared password if and when they break up.

Teen love is intoxicating, addictive, and all-consuming. Teens in love will do ANYTHING to prove their love to the chosen one! In today's world, the pressure to share a password is almost greater than the pressure to have sex! Sharing passwords (not saliva) is the ultimate test of true love. Unfortunately, due to inexperience, teens think that love lasts forever and are shocked and surprised when this gift of intimacy gets turned against them after a breakup.

Intimate Facebook messages and emails that profess love in sexual language or supposedly confidential conversations about other people can spread like wildfire through the friend community. Oh, the humiliation! It's not only talk between lovers that is exposed to unintended audiences, but also messages and emails from other people, including you. Perhaps you've written a heartfelt private email or text to your son in which you share your worries about his current love interest. Unbeknownst to you, that person is now privy to your conversations with your child. Also, that girlfriend now can read emails and messages from friends who may be sharing intimacies that they don't want shared with anyone else. Perhaps a new crush sends a message trying to gauge interest, not knowing the girlfriend is also reading. There are so many unanticipated complications, and so much potential heartache, from just one secret word.

Here's the Solution

Just telling your teen not to share passwords is not a helpful strategy in the moment when a beloved or a best friend makes the password request. Not wanting to disappoint or in any way convey mistrust to these special people, a teen will willingly and without pause share a password. Teens need help in understanding all the consequences of sharing passwords and, even more important, what to say that lets them off the hook without looking like they don't love or trust the person asking. This is a delicate situation. Parents need to understand just how hard it is to say no. A big worry for teens is that saying no will forever damage this coveted and special relationship.

As always, it's important to come from a place of understanding, not judgment. The following is NOT a conversation starter: "I hope you haven't given out your passwords to your email, phone, or Facebook accounts. That is really stupid. You can't trust your friends to keep it private." Here is what your teen heard: "You are stupid and your friends are untrustworthy." It's unlikely that the conversation will go any further. Your teen will become angry and will shut down.

Instead, it might go this way: "I read recently that kids are sharing their passwords with their boyfriends and girlfriends. I get that that must be a true sign of trust and love to share all of your private conversations with other people in your life. In the moment when they ask, I'm guessing it would be really hard to say no because you would want them to know that you trust them and that you have nothing to hide. What you might not think of is that sometimes your friends or even we will write things to you that are meant only for you. I know I wouldn't want anyone reading some of the stuff that I've written to you. I bet your friends confide in you a lot. I don't think they would want anybody else reading that stuff. It's probably pretty personal and could be embarrassing or cause problems if other people read it. Maybe your best friend writes to you about cheating on her boyfriend, and your boyfriend is her boyfriend's best friend. After he reads the message she sent you, he might feel he needs to give his friend the heads-up. They break up, all because you gave your boyfriend your password to your private messages. It's tempting, I know! If you had your boyfriend's password, wouldn't you be tempted to read what he writes and know who writes to him? I know I would. And finally, when people are in love they write all kinds of private things to each other. But when there's a breakup and feelings are hurt, what's to keep the injured party from making public stuff that was read and sent in private? I know this is a lot, and it's really hard to think about.

"Maybe you've already been put in this position, and maybe you haven't, but let me help you come up with something that you could say that would make the other person not feel rejected or hurt. You could say, 'You know I love you, and it's so sweet that you want us to share everything. But just like I like to keep private what you and I write and send to each other, I like to do that with my friends. My friends confide in me very personal things, and I know they wouldn't like knowing that you would be reading their stuff. I hope you understand.'"

File this under "Why Does Parenting a Teenager Have to Be So Hard?"

cleaning up facebook and twitter posts

preparing your teen for the real world of jobs and college

Here's the Problem

The accessibility of complete and total strangers to anything you put out in the world of social media gives the proverbial "fly on the wall" metaphor a whole new meaning. Some of these total strangers are potential employers, college admissions officers, directors of internship programs; the list goes on. According to a Microsoft survey, close to 80 percent of employers check out prospective job applicants' online profiles, and 70 percent have rejected candidates because profiles and posts contain unseemly language, photos, or just plain unlikable material. Let the parent lectures begin!

Why It's a Problem

Teens who are thinking about a cool summer job or internship need to beware. How about looking to become a camp counselor? Perhaps the camp director is social media savvy and goes on your teen's Facebook (you know how selective teens are about friending people) or on Tumblr, Twitter, or Instagram to nose around. If your teen has been posting obscenity-laden quips, stories of drunken exploits, or sexually explicit photos, it may turn off a camp director who's looking for wholesome counselors. Perhaps your teen is vying for a highly competitive internship, and the director of the program is looking for Mr. or Ms. Responsible? I don't think the director will be impressed by a post that begins, "Man I got wasted and . . ."

Another potential scenario: Your teen is waiting to hear from colleges. This is a tough college market, and that admissions director's decision may come down to what she found during her social media sleuthing!

This is definitely not something that's on your teen's radar. Teens are having way too much fun posting things that are crazy, silly, gross, and provocative. After all, they have all their "fans" to entertain. The absolute furthest thing from their minds is the future, even a "future" that is only weeks or months away. Remember, teens live in the present, but their parents live in the future. Parents are their teen's very own crystal balls!

Here's the Solution

Your teens will need you to do some thinking ahead for them. Here's a conversation parents might have: "You know honey, I get that posting outrageous stuff on your Facebook, Instagram, and Twitter is fun, but the reality is that it makes your life an open book to college admissions people and potential job and internship employers. I read an article recently that all those people look at an applicant's social networking posts to see what kind of person they are when they think adults aren't watching. Kids have actually been rejected from jobs and schools because of the kinds of things they post. I wouldn't want something like the stuff you put out there in Internet Land to get in the way of doing what you want. I think it's time to do some 'housecleaning.' As you go through all your postings, think like a potential boss or admissions director and ask:

→ What impression am I getting about this student or employee from their social network pages? You wouldn't want them to say, 'Wow, this kid seems to party a lot, which would probably affect his ability to work' or 'He uses a lot of sexually explicit language; he doesn't show much respect for women and I wouldn't want him interacting with my staff.'

→ Look at postings from your friends. Anything there that someone could think of as 'guilt by association'? Look at photos where you're tagged, and sexually provocative posts or obscene language. Delete those posts. Here is how: Go to your Facebook timeline, hover over the offending post, and a menu will drop down. Click on 'remove' or 'delete.' Done!"

Help your teens to ask the right questions and then send them on their way with a Mr. Clean power eraser!

online bullying
being made fun of can really hurt

Here's the Problem

According to an Associated Press–MTV poll, 56 percent of teens have experienced some type of online taunting, harassment, or bullying. This is an astounding, disturbing, and scary statistic. Teens complained that there were false rumors spread about them or that people took photos or videos of them and posted them without their permission. And let's just say these photos or videos did not show them in the most flattering light. One of the most egregious examples occurred in Ohio where a video was filmed and posted of high school football players raping an extremely intoxicated high school girl. Needless to say, that girl's life has been forever changed.

Why It's a Problem

Eighty percent of all teens are cyber-connected. There's a high likelihood that your teen will either be the target of cyberbullying or will be the bully. Spreading rumors and exacting revenge has always been a staple of teen relationships. When I was a teen growing up in the 1960s teenagers were mean to one another too. We spread rumors about one another and "got back" at those we thought had wronged us. The good news then was that the incident vanished as soon as another took its place. It was still painful being the target, but by the end of the week, you were forgotten the moment someone else had the target on her back. This gave valuable time to recover from the humiliation.

For today's teens, the humiliation never ends. An issue that might have just been between two people now becomes fun fodder for thousands, thanks to multiple outlets of shame. Things can get reposted to any number of sites, and by any number of people. When revenge or humiliation is in the air, look out!

I worked with a parent who was stunned when she got a call from the principal informing her that her daughter had been involved in a cyberbullying incident. It seems that an overweight, socially awkward student at the school, who had regularly been the target of bullying, was sitting and reading in a study carrel in the school library, minding his own business. Unbeknownst to him, someone took a photo of him with their phone and posted it on Facebook with a caption making fun of him. It wasn't long before many kids joined "the fun," each one trying to out-outrageous the previous comments. Many of these kids, including this woman's daughter, didn't even know the boy but got caught up in the competition to write the "funniest" post. The boy himself was long forgotten in the feeding frenzy of posting. No one was thinking how he might feel. It was just an "awesome good time."

Technology is the perfect bullying delivery system. Saying something to someone's face takes courage and conviction. Writing an anonymous post with no fear of consequence is risk-free.

In a Federal Youth Risk Behavior Study of 15,425 teens, 3,416 reported that they had been cyberbullied. Of those kids, 1,708 (50 percent) had not told their parents. Nearly half of those kids (785) said that because of the anxiety and depression they had considered suicide.

Many teens suffering the consequences of cyberbullying are not going to their parents for help. Some see no way out and consider suicide as their only option. Teens resist getting help from their parents. One obstacle is worrying that it's "babyish" for Mom and Dad to help them with something they should be able to handle on their own. An even bigger worry is that if they tell their parents what's going on, they'll jump into action, call the principal and other authorities, and make a bad problem worse. Better not to tell!

Here's the Solution

First, it's important to acknowledge that yes, even your teen, the one you have raised to be a kind, thoughtful person, might engage in cyberbullying. Understand that with technology, bullying takes on a crowd mentality. All teens are vulnerable. Many are both victims *and* bullies. This isn't about good kids vs. bad kids. It's about self-conscious, impulsive teens getting caught up in moments for which they are not prepared.

Your teens need you to help them navigate these stormy waters. Start by opening up a conversation. Scour the newspapers or look online for stories about teens and bullying. With a few of these articles in hand, let your teen know that you know this is a major issue in a teen's life. Don't go on the lecture circuit. Instead, ask general questions like, "I get that this must go on at your school; it must be so hard to deal with. Do you know anyone this has happened to?" Hopefully since you are really just listening, your teen will feel free to share a story or two. Then you might say, "I get that kids do this stuff, and I know that you are a kind and thoughtful person and probably don't want to get caught up in this frenzy, but it must be hard not to when kids see this as normal. I know that what people think about you feels so important, and that you might feel the need to participate in things you don't want to so your friends will think you're 'one of them.' I know this must be so hard sometimes. I want to be able to help you with this stuff. I promise I won't get mad or call anyone's parents. I just want to help you get out of a situation you get stuck in before it goes sour."

Make sure your teens know that if they are victims of bullying, the earlier they tell you about it the more you can help. Promise not to contact the principal or the bully's parents. You will just have to develop some strategies to make it better. Obviously, if the bullying is persistent and threatening, you must contact the school.

If you have been monitoring your teen's Facebook, Twitter, Instagram, and Ask.fm posts, you will likely have a heads-up. That's why monitoring is so important. If you begin to see some mean stuff on there, you can have your teen block these posts. You can "hide" particular people's posts without unfriending them on Facebook. Teens can unfollow those kids on Twitter who bully them and can block them from posting on their Twitter feed. Help your teen to understand that "out of sight, out of mind" is a great survival tool. If you don't know what someone is saying about you, then you can't feel bad about it.

Bullies get their power from making people feel and act like victims. Most victims of cyberbullying feel completely helpless to make it stop. Give your teen a boost in self-confidence and personal power. These are a bully's worst enemies.

four ways of fighting
a roadmap for effective arguing

Here's the Problem

Say you go to your teen with a request to do something, go somewhere, or "process" some issue you feel you need to "work through" with him. Either way you state your case in a kind and clear manner, hoping to ward off an argument. Your teen does not agree. You begin to feel defensive as your teen accuses you of being overprotective, overbearing, too strict, and the worst parent ever. It's tough not to get hooked. Let the battle begin!

Teaching your teen to resolve conflict in a respectful way is a life skill. What model does your family practice? Duking it out until everybody is either slamming doors or in tears, or avoiding conflict altogether, are not productive or healthy ways to resolve conflict. How you do it will be the model your teens take with them into adulthood as they navigate relationships. So take a good hard look at what you've been modeling and teaching your children about conflict resolution.

Why It's a Problem

Arguing with a teen can get loud and it can get mean. It can get ugly! Like any good fight, both parties are motivated to win. Parents fear a loss of respect and control if *they* lose, and teens feel a loss of their newly found feelings of independence if *they* lose.

Arguing actually serves a developmental purpose in adolescence. For teens who are just learning to separate from Mom and Dad and think for themselves, arguing with their parents is a way for them to shout from the rooftops that "I'M NOT YOU!" Additionally, a teen's brain is wired differently than an adult's. The amygdala, or the emotional center of the brain, is much more active in teens than is the thinking center, or frontal cortex. Once the amygdala is activated and firing on all cylinders, it's pretty hard to shut down. Think of a stovetop burner that's been on high. Once you shut it off, it takes a good amount of time before you can touch it without being burned. Such is the amygdala of the teenage brain.

If you can blame your teen's overreaction on biology rather than on something he has some control over, you'll be less likely to label him as spoiled and disrespectful. Negative feelings like these are destructive to the relationship, interfering with the ability to resolve the conflict. Resolution should always be the ultimate goal.

Here's the Solution

There's no one-size-fits-all in the world of parent-teen conflict. Different kinds of arguments require different strategies. Below are four of the most common parent-teen fights and the specific strategies that I recommend.

Fight 1

OK, so sometimes teens are snarky and sarcastic. They make fun of you, your clothes, your job, your cooking—just like a bully. This actually isn't as mean-spirited as it seems. Here's why: Your teen's newly updated brain is now able to perform the skill of analysis. She's literally having thoughts about you she's never had before. Prior to this delightful stage, your child saw you as perfection personified. Sure, you might have been unfair sometimes by not letting her eat an extra snack or stay up a little later, but basically, you were her number 1! Moving into adolescence and this newer brain model, your teen is now capable of seeing all your imperfections and moments of hypocrisy. It's fun to see that your parents are capable of the same kinds of mistakes that you make! And your teen wants to make sure that you know it. Hello sarcasm! But fear not. You can reframe this by acknowledging that having a teen is like having your very own free, in-house psychologist. Perhaps their "feedback" about you could be helpful and reveal something about yourself you may be unaware of. Sometimes this feedback just feels mean-spirited and hurtful, and you react with anger and hurt. "How dare you be so disrespectful!" you may scream at your teen. If this is how you respond to some of these "gotcha" moments, it's a thumbs-up for your teen. *"I have the power to make the all-powerful parent feel bad. Score!"*

Instead, fight this sarcasm with humor. Don't give them the power to hurt your feelings. You don't want to give a "bully" any power. Instead, after one of those mean comments, offer a huge hug and say, "You are just so cute when you're trying to be a bully." You want to catch your teen off guard with your love. But your message really is, "No way are you getting away with trying to make me feel small!"

Fight 2

There are many times you must say no to your teen. Some requests are unsafe or unreasonable. I know there are many other times that you say no to your teen. I'm not talking about the knee-jerk no when your teen has caught you off guard in the middle of something, or you're just so dog tired that you're hoping that no will be a conversation stopper. I'm not talking about that no.

Your teen has asked, in her usual impulsive, not-having-thought-it-through way, for permission to go somewhere, get something, or do something. You are clear on this: NO. You have no ambivalence whatsoever. There is no room for compromise here. You say "no" and give your teen a reasonable explanation for your decision, and still all hell breaks loose. Your teen has already given herself permission in her own head, and your no is in direct contradiction to her inner dialogue, so she goes ballistic. This draws you into a defensive and lecturing posture. Again and again, you attempt to give her a reasonable rationale. Unfortunately, she stopped listening at no. Let the fighting begin.

Instead, try this. Because YOU are so clear on your no, you have no need to get defensive. This leaves you free to be on your teen's side by understanding her disappointment. Instead of saying, "Well, this is my answer and if you don't like it you can go find another family!" you can say, "I get that you're ticked at me, and I get that you're disappointed. I know it must be hard to see your friends do something that we don't think is safe. I get it." And that's it. Do not say another word! Give a shoulder shrug, which is the period at the end of your sentence. There really is nothing left to say. You have stated your case, and you have empathized and understood her disappointment. Having realistic expectations here is key. When your teen hears no to something that has been a yes in her head, she will not thank you for the wonderful parenting decision. She'll be mad, and understandably so. You have crushed a dream of . . . whatever the dream was. It's OK to let your teen be mad without having to get mad back.

Fight 3

More often than not, your teen knows exactly how to push your buttons and can take you from 0 to 100 in a nanosecond. Or maybe you're a bit of a control freak and like to have the last word, in any argument, not just one with your teen. In both cases an argument with your teen gets way out of control. In these situations both parties tend to forget what actually started the fight and move on to what a bad parent you are (from your teen's point of view) or what an ungrateful, rude, disrespectful teen he is (from your point of view)! There are no winners in this fight and no resolution. There are times that everyone loses it even with the best-laid plans. You're tired, overworked, and stressed to the max, and when your teen pushes your buttons, you lose control. I hope this strategy will help you in those situations.

Your first task is to recognize when you've lost it. Are you screaming? Are veins pulsing out of your neck? This does require some on-the-spot self-reflection, but trust me, practicing it makes it easier. You recognize this and say as calmly as humanly possible, "We're both out of control, and we need to take a break." And that is what you do: Do not tell your teen to leave the room. YOU LEAVE! And don't make the mistake of just moving into another room; your teen will follow you and wear you down until you say yes. Leave the house if you can. Walk the dog. Get a coffee. Sit in your car! If this doesn't seem possible then at least go to your bedroom and close the door. Some relentless teens will follow you to your room and barge in, looking for a "yes"! If your teen doesn't respect your boundaries, rather than getting into a fight about it, calmly say, "I'm going to take a shower now and will be getting naked momentarily. Hope you don't mind." Then start to disrobe. Your teen will run for the hills. Trust me, no teen wants to even think about their parent naked!

Take whatever time you need to calm yourself. Then go to your teen and say, "I really would like to hear what you have to say." Now it's your job to listen. Don't start back in again with the same lecture you left off with. That will just get the fight going again. Now that your teen has calmed down as well, you might not actually hear the crazy, impulsive demands you heard in round one. Maybe there will be some room for compromise now that every-one is listening. Then again, maybe not. Maybe, as in Fight 2, the request is unsafe or unreasonable. In this case, do as in Fight 2: Empathize with your teen's disappointment, give a shoulder shrug, and walk away!

Fight 4

This is perhaps the most upsetting of the fights you will have with your teen. The other three are not always fun, but they are an expected and a normal part of the parent-teen relationship. This last fight occurs when your teen has crossed the line by saying something seriously hurtful and disrespectful. Perhaps they have screamed, "I hate you!" or even "F**k you!" or something similar. This is absolutely not acceptable. Not ever!

You might be surprised at first when you start to read the following strat-egy. Most parents, when confronted with sentiments or language like that, scream back, "You do not talk to me like that!" Except they already have! At this point, parents will often take away anything and everything they think will "teach that kid a lesson." Gone goes the cellphone, the computer. The teen is grounded and who knows what else. The problem with this type of reaction is that it doesn't really address the relationship.

In this approach, you do the unexpected. After your teen spews, you look him calmly in the eye and say without yelling, "I can't believe that you would say something like that to me." And that's all you say. You turn and walk away. Your teen, expecting an all-out battle, will be shocked. Don't allow yourself to be drawn into the fray. Remember that teens actually like the fight. I want you to deprive yours of that release.

Here is the most important consequence for your teen. It is not losing the phone or the computer or being grounded. Now, you wait until the next time your teen comes to you and asks for a ride, money, help with homework, to go to Staples, whatever. And believe me, it will happen, if not that night then the next morning. Your teen needs and gets a lot from you. And let's face it, that's what parents do, they help their kids. But this time you say, calmly and without attitude, "You know honey, I would have loved to drive you or to help you today, but since you said [repeat whatever he said] I really don't feel that I want to do that for you today."

It's important here not to be sarcastic or to sound childish. By using this approach you are teaching your teen that relationships are reciprocal. When you're disrespected and hurt by someone, you don't want to do the things that normally would be acts of kindness and love.

I had a parent do this once after a particularly abusive incident with her teenage daughter. This mother usually drove her daughter to school every morning, even though it was only a mile walk. The mother loved doing this for her daughter because she knew it gave her a few extra minutes in that tough early-morning time. After a horrible battle the previous evening when the daughter became abusive, the mom decided that she would not drive her daughter to school. In the morning, the daughter had completely forgotten the fight and was ready for Mom to drive her. The daughter, seeing that Mom was not dressed or moving toward the car, said, "Mom, I have to get to school, come on." And the mom calmly said, "You know honey, I love driving you to school, but last night when you screamed _____ at me, I was very hurt and now I really don't feel like helping you out today." The daughter was stunned. And of course she denied the fight and denied the abuse. I had coached Mom not to say another word. The daughter walked to school. All day long the daughter texted her mom, apologizing profusely. It was the first time this mom had taken a stand for herself. And it worked!

Arguing with your teen is hard, and it's exhausting. But it's a necessary and important part of your relationship.

70 puh-leez . . . no lecture

Here's the Problem

I'm sure this takes place in your household at least once a day. Your teen says something provocative, narcissistic, or naive. Thinking that you need to "set him straight," you respond with a lecture about why what he said is unrealistic. I worked with a couple that was regularly getting hooked into these kinds of conversations with their 15-year-old son. Their relationship with him was deteriorating. They were frustrated with his inability to be realistic, and he was frustrated with their inability to understand him. He would regularly announce his plans for "when he grew up" or taunt his parents' political views or accuse them of being hypocrites about their lifestyle. I don't remember exactly what he wanted to do, but the conversation went something like this:

Teen: I want to be a rock star!

Parent: How can you be a rock star if you don't play the guitar, can't sing, and hate to practice or put time into anything?

Teen: You just don't understand that music is my passion!

Why It's a Problem

Adolescence is about fantasy. It's about seeing all the new possibilities that life has to offer. It's about idealism and unrealistic expectations. For the first time in their lives, they're thinking with a new brain that literally floods them with endless thoughts, ideas, and plans, most of which they will discard naturally as they experience life. They actually don't need your "realism" because they'll find out for themselves from living life and from experiencing disappointment and disillusionment when real life doesn't imitate fantasy life. In some ways teens are playing the "dress-up" games of early childhood. They're metaphorically trying on those cowboy or princess costumes. They'll eventually outgrow the games and get on with life.

Another couple I worked with made the mistake of taking every conversation or idea their teen had as a reality that needed a plan. So when their teen said she loved to bake, they lectured her about applying to culinary school and what a career in baking would be like. Truthfully, she just liked baking brownies. Every time their teen expressed an interest or a musing about something, they felt it was their responsibility to act on it and "show her the way." Their teen stopped talking to them, sick of having to listen to them be so serious about a future that was many years away.

Here's the Solution

You don't need to be worried or feel the need to tell them how it really is. They'll figure it out on their own. Your job is just to say, "Yeah, I get how much fun that would be" or "Great goal. Let me know how I can help" or "I'm not sure I agree, but I understand why you would think that." Your kids are just thinking out loud. The edit button is not firmly in place yet. Most of us have silly things in our head or fantasies about winning the lottery or Publishers Clearing House sweepstakes, but we keep those thoughts to ourselves. Otherwise people would think we're nuts! If you don't give them the room and the opportunity to say things out loud, free of judgment and criticism, you run the risk that they will anticipate your "discouraging word" and shut you out. If you do give them "editorial freedom," eventually they'll ask for your help and your opinion. They'll value it because you have allowed them the opportunity to give voice to their own thoughts. Teens are playing out all the options and choices they will have to make over the next 10 years. The operative word is "play." Don't "show" them how to finish a puzzle. Give them the pieces and let them figure it out!

71 playing the game of curfew

"please can I? everybody else is"

Here's the Problem

Remember when your teens were young children and their bedtime battle cry of "Just five more minutes pleeese?" was a nightly ritual? Fast-forward 10 years and the battle cry is still there, but now it's curfew: "Just one more hour pleeese?"

A parent shared this story with me. Her 16-year-old daughter was off to a party. The agreed-upon curfew was 11:15 p.m. The ride home was prearranged, and a call to the home of the party had confirmed that parents would be home supervising. All was well in the land. Mom and Dad, confident that the plan for the night was in place, awaited their daughter's return. At precisely 11:15 p.m. the phone rang. "Hi guys, can I sleep over? Everyone's sleeping over, pleeese!!!" Mom and Dad were not pleased. The "everybody else's parents says it's all right" defense never played well with them. And they weren't happy that she waited until the exact minute she was to be home to call with the request. There was a resounding NO from the parental unit. The posturing went on for some time. There was arguing, and the "you'd better get your a** home" capped off the multiple phone calls. The daughter finally returned home an hour later than the agreed-upon curfew. The parents, too tired to deal with consequences, took their daughter's cellphone away and were prepared to ground her for a time to be determined.

Why It's a Problem

Why is it that teens can't seem to be on top of this time thing and wait until the last minute to inform or request changes? Sometimes it's because they're truly unaware of time, living wholly in the moment. Sometimes it's because they know that when they wait until the last minute, you will have fewer options and they'll have a better chance to get what they want. Either you cave to the "everybody else's parents say it's OK" or you tell them to get their a**es home. But either way they've stayed out later than the agreed-upon time, and you've been played.

Here's the Solution

Let your teen know that if she waits to call you for curfew or plan adjustments until the time she was supposed to be home, the answer will always be no. This makes life simple. If she calls you at least 30 minutes before the previously agreed-upon time, you'll at least listen to the request. You can say to your teen, "I get that plans change, and that you may need some adjustment on when you need to get home. But if you choose to wait until the time you're supposed to be home to call and ask, I'll always say no. You need to give me some notice, at least 30 minutes. If you call me at curfew time, the answer will be no, and however late you are for curfew, you will be docked next time out." If this system had been in place, the daughter would have had to call by 10:45 for the request to have even been considered.

Curfew times should in general be fluid to avoid this kind of interaction altogether. Many parents I have worked with have a rigid curfew no matter what the circumstances. Different evening activities require different time frames. Flexibility helps to set your teen up for "curfew success." For example, setting an 11:15 curfew on a night that your teen decides to go to a 9:30 movie is a setup for "curfew failure."

It's not only important to set a curfew to get your teen home at a reasonable hour, but also, more important, curfews teach teens to be responsible for their behavior. This isn't just for when they are teenagers but also as they move into adulthood. Consideration and responsibility are qualities you hope your teen develops in abundance. How many adults do you know who are always late for dinner or always changing plans with you at the last minute? I'm guessing that as teens they were not held accountable for their time, and now they feel free to make and keep their own timetables. This is not only about taking control as a parent, but also about teaching consideration.

72 ask less, get more
stop the interrogation

Here's the Problem

"You're so annoying!" "Stop asking me so many questions!" "Stop texting me every five minutes!" Sound familiar? I'm guessing that at least once a day, after another "interview" with your teen that's gone awry, you feel the door being metaphorically shut in your face. What went wrong? You ran down your checklist, question by question with your teen, hoping and praying you'd find out something about his day and his life. The college students I've surveyed, and the countless teens I have counseled and talked to, cite the "nosiness" of their parents as being their most irritating quality. The irony is that as your kids move into adolescence, the more you need to know so you can keep them on track and safe, the less they want to talk to you. And of course, the less they want to talk to you, the more questions you ask! It's a vicious cycle where no one wins. Your teen gets bombarded with a million questions, and you get no information.

Why It's a Problem

Sometimes you ask questions when you're worried. Maybe your teen walks in after school with his head and shoulders drooping, and you just know something is up. You ask how his day was and you get the grunt, "Fine." Your antenna goes up. He doesn't sound fine. So you go a little further: "Did something happen?" "Did you get your project back?" "Did you have a fight with one of your friends?" And you keep on going, hoping one of your questions will be the right one and your teen will spill.

Unfortunately, it goes the other way, and either your teen stays silent or screams, "Leave me alone!" and bolts to the safety of his room. You're left with your anger at his attitude and silence, while simultaneously racked with fear that something is wrong but you don't know what, and you can't fix it.

In this scenario it may be that a million things are wrong, none of them major, but all together it feels dreadful. Your teen can't answer your questions because he doesn't know! It may be an accumulation of things that began at 6:30 a.m. with a bad hair day, followed by an embarrassing gaffe answering a question in English, followed by a tripping incident in the hallway in front of 300 kids, and so on. Get the picture?

A lot of parental interrogation concerns the minutiae of a teen's daily life: "What do you have for homework?" "Where are you going?" "Who are you going with?" "When were you planning on doing your homework, your chores, your SAT review?"

Maybe your interrogation tactic is to bombard your teen with texts when he's out with his friends, wanting to make sure he doesn't forget what's "really important." But all you get back is the virtual "cold shoulder."

Parents are information junkies. Beginning with babysitters and preschool teachers, parents are fed a daily diet of the nitty-gritty of their child's life. From what toys and which kids they played with, to what they ate for lunch, to how many times they peed and pooped. When their children moved on to elementary school, it took only a single question: "How was school today?" And the kids gave an enthusiastic and detailed recitation of their day. The parental addiction to information was fed and nourished.

Now as their children enter adolescence, parents are forced to go "cold turkey." Not only do questions go unanswered, but now they're also criticized and sneered at for even asking them! As teens move toward increased independence, information becomes more scant and on a need-to-know basis. The more questions parents ask, the less information they get. It's time for a change of tactics.

Here's the Solution

First of all, timing is everything. Do not start your interrogation the second your teen walks in the door! Teens are emotionally and mentally exhausted at the end of the day, and unless they're in the best mood ever, I can guarantee that you'll get the silent treatment or the grunt, "Fine!" If you sense something worrisome in his voice or body language, give him some time alone to recoup. Later, stop in his room and make a statement or observation like, "You seem like you had a tough day today. Anything I can do to help?" Maybe there's nothing you can do. You'll just have to leave it alone, as hard as that is. Sometimes your teen wants to figure it out for himself. That's how resilience is built. You have to be attuned to your teen's mood. If he's giving off obvious don't-talk-to-me body language, then it's not the time for conversation. You'll only be disappointed and feel rejection, which eventually turns into anger.

Second, rip up your checklist! Try to keep it to one general question about homework or weekend plans rather than 10 detailed ones. A casual "So what's up for tonight?" feels much less invasive than "How much homework do you have?" "Do you have a quiz to study for?" "When is that project due?" For questions about weekend time spent out of the house, you might make a statement: "Before you leave I'll need to know the usual information." Or a casual "So what are you guys up to tonight?" Most teens will want to share information with you, but will withhold it when they feel your desperation. That makes it another power struggle for them to win. You might say, "I get that I probably annoy you by asking you a million questions. Here's the thing. I miss you. I just want to know what's going on with you. Is there a better way we can do this?"

Some teens are uncomfortable with excessive face time with their parents. You can always text or email. They can take only so much of your longing, puppy-dog looks or irritated looks and comments. Some kids are better writers than talkers.

Take them out for coffee or an ice cream, play a video game with them, or watch their favorite TV show with them and talk during commercials. All of these will probably get you more info than a 25-point checklist.

The bottom line is you can't make them talk. You want them to want to talk with you. And that takes finesse, humor, and patience.

too much love can be a bad thing

holding your teen accountable

Here's the Problem

On a recent flight back from the West Coast, I sat with a lovely couple who thankfully kept me occupied with conversation for five hours, distracting me from my fear of flying. In the course of the conversation we covered all the usual stuff: who we were visiting, where we were from, and what we did for a living. On hearing I was a parenting expert, and with an encouraging nod from me, we settled into a coaching session about their 27-year-old son. These clearly loving and lovely parents were distraught about the failings of this young man. It seems this guy was the golden child growing up: talented athlete, popular and adored by both adults and peers, and a good student. Off he went to college, where I'm guessing his golden-boy status fell on deaf ears in a large university setting. No longer the big fish in a small pond and with no "adoring fans," just fellow students, he entered the real world. He started with smoking pot, but more recently he was found to have an addiction to OxyContin. He has managed to hold a job, but his drug habit has put him thousands of dollars into debt. He has totaled two cars and crashed a third and is now financially dependent on his parents, who continually bail him out. He's allowed to live rent-free in the downstairs apartment of the two-family house they own. His parents pay his phone bill and car insurance; they buy his groceries and do his laundry. They rescue him from most of the trouble he finds himself in. Peter Pan couldn't have said it better: "I won't grow up."

Why It's a Problem

There's no question that these parents are loving, attentive, and supportive and have always been engaged and involved in their children's lives. But this is a case study of too much involvement and is a cautionary tale for all parents. This dad is the "fixer." He loves feeling needed, and he jumps at the chance to solve problems for his kids. He's the car buyer, the job finder, and the bill payer. Mom is the "nurturer." Nothing makes her happier than doing for her kids, whether it's their cooking, cleaning, or their laundry. These are two wonderful parents.

But here's the trouble. As an adult, rather than being appreciative and grateful for all his parents do for him, this man now feels entitled and dependent on them. This young man has been so taken care of that he has no motivation to do it for himself. And frankly, who can blame him? If he knows that Mom and Dad will be there to rescue him from responsibility no matter what, why be responsible at all?

What's less obvious is that this young man probably feels like a loser. Yes, it's nice to have a fancy car, a state-of-the-art phone, and free digs, but all *his* money goes to his drug dealers, and his parents support this lifestyle. This is not self-esteem-building behavior. Though on the outside it may look like he's in "fat city," he knows that this is not where he should be at 27, with Mom cooking and doing his laundry and Dad paying all his bills. Normally, we want our kids to grow up to be independent, which is what they want for themselves as well.

Here's the Solution

In the not-so-distant future your teens will be young adults. Your job is to help them develop the skills *now* that they will need as they enter the world on their own. Here are some strategies to prepare them for becoming responsible adults in the future.

Do not "overhelp" with their schoolwork. No one is entitled to a college education. If your high school student is not showing academic motivation and you find yourself the "orchestrator" of homework, papers, and projects, this can be a red flag for future school success. Doing it for them inhibits their ability to develop skills in time management, manage frustration when the work is hard, or feel responsible for their successes and failures. Be clear with your expectations. "I get that you hate doing homework, but here's the thing: no work, no college."

Make your teens have to work for some things. Kids do not "need" state-of-the-art phones, computers, clothes, video games, and all the other nonessentials of life. Many teens have come to expect that they should have the "best of everything." But you know what builds self-esteem, self-confidence, and resilience? Not being given to, but working for!

Resist the temptation to be the problem solver and say, "Here's what I think you should do." Better to say, "Well, what do *you* think you should do?" Don't find your teen a summer job or an internship. Do not write her college essays or make her college lists. If you do everything, she'll never get to have that feeling of "Look what I did, I'm so proud of myself!" Instead, you get to feel "Look what a great parent I am!" But it's more important for your teen to feel that sense of accomplishment than for you. It's also important for her to learn the steps for effective problem solving. Your role is to guide her through this process and empower her with your confidence as she does the work herself.

Becoming an independent adult takes training. Doing for them does not build independence. Adolescence is the time to teach.

74

too much, too soon
understanding age-appropriate privileges

Here's the Problem

Remember when you were a little kid and you wanted to stay up later, get your ears pierced, own a bigger or fancier bike, wear certain kinds of clothes, or see certain kinds of movies? Your parents would say, "When you're older you'll be able to _____." As children we looked forward to those "markers" that signified a move toward "being old enough to _____." Rites of passage and markers that suggest maturity define leaving one stage behind and moving on to another. Adolescence offers the opportunity to experience new and different kinds of activities, take on new responsibilities, and experience new kinds of relationships.

Lately, it seems there are fewer and fewer of these markers. Just 10 years ago, you might have bought a personal computer for your child as a high-school-graduation/going-away-to-college gift. Signifying achievement and moving forward, it was an important psychological marker. Now most teens have their own laptop by the age of 12. It used to be that when teens got their driver's licenses, they were happy just to be driving whatever they could get their hands on, the clunkier the better; grandma's old car was perfect. Now while visiting high schools, I see teens driving around in cars I still aspire to own, the hottest and newest model on the market!

Why It's a Problem

There are few things left for our kids to aspire to. We used to have clothing markers, privilege markers, and music markers. They served a purpose. They helped slow down time and allow kids to enjoy and learn the lessons of childhood before they moved into the confusing world of adolescence. There was a sense of excitement over what was to come.

Now it's sex and music, clothes and technology, alcohol and drugs, all with kids too young to understand their significance. A parent asked me whether she was being ridiculous when her 11-year-old daughter, a fifth grader, asked to go to a Saturday night "boy-girl" party and she said no. I applauded her decision. A bowling party, a roller-skating or ice-skating party, these are structured, safe, and appropriate kinds of parties for the tween-age crowd. They respect tweens' growing curiosity and excitement about the opposite sex, but provide a safe and comfortable setting in which to explore these new kinds of relationships. But a down-in-the-basement kind of party, that's a whole other ball game! With kids too immature to feel comfortable in this kind of intimate setting, there's a pressure to "act like teenagers." But since they're not actually teenagers yet, they have to imitate the ones they know: older siblings, babysitters, and the cool kids they see on TV and in movies. With these "teens" as their models, they engage in behavior unbecoming to 11-year-olds, such as playing kissing games and drinking alcohol they've lifted from their parents' liquor cabinets, all with parents upstairs in the living room, naive enough to think nothing's going on!

Smartphones and iPads with unlimited access to the Internet and potentially dangerous information; unsupervised and unlimited tweeting, texting, Instagram, Vine, Ask.fm, Snapchat; unsupervised get-togethers; personal laptops in the bedroom. These are freedoms that should come with age and maturity.

Here's the Solution

There's value in understanding that we don't get everything we want when we want it. Some things *are* worth waiting for, and when they do come we appreciate them even more. Remember, teens live in the moment. It's the adults in their lives who need to help them to look toward the future. That old-fashioned work ethic our forefathers and foremothers taught our parents—that nothing is just given to you and if you want something you have to work hard for it—seems to have gotten lost in translation, along with "You're just not old enough." It's OK to say no to your kids. It's OK to say, "These things cost a lot of money, and that's not how we choose to spend it." It's OK to say, "What you have is enough!" And it's OK to say, "You're just not old enough." This is not easy to do. Many parents succumb to the pressure of "everybody else is" from their teens, or perhaps they want to be the "cool" parents and stay on trend, or want their teen to be on the cutting edge of technology. But most troubling is that parents haven't thought through the consequences of a yes to their demanding teen. That's their job! The ability to think things through and anticipate probable consequences is not a realistic expectation of your teen. But it's a realistic expectation that you should have for yourself. So the next time your teen comes to you wanting to do something or buy something that feels to you like it's not age-appropriate, it probably isn't. Learning to trust your gut is one of the most valuable tools you have as a parent. It's OK to be an old fuddy-duddy. I'm one, and I'm proud of it!

"so what, who cares?"
making consequences mean something

75

Here's the Problem

So what, who cares? These could be the most irritating four words a teen ever utters. Teens refuse to do what is asked of them; they flout rules that Mom and Dad thought had been agreed upon. They get report cards with less-than-stellar grades even though they had sworn up and down they had pulled their grades up.

So you give your teen a consequence that you hope will mean something. You want to teach a lesson so that the next time XYZ happens, your kid will think first of the consequence of doing the wrong thing.

You hope and expect to hear anger and moans and groans. This means that at the least, you've "gotten" to your teen and perhaps have taught your teen a lesson. But "So what, who cares?" pushes your buttons and sets you off your well-laid course. Off you go to the land of "Argumentamia." Your teen has played the game well and has seemingly taken away all your power.

Why It's a Problem

It may be that your teen responds in that way because he knows you, and he knows that the consequences you put into play are often forgotten about (or reversed if he can make a good argument). Or perhaps he's just trying to goad you into a bigger argument, knowing how best to push your buttons. Or maybe he really doesn't care. A mom told me of a situation with her 12-year-old son whose attitude was out of control. At her wit's end, she took away his Xbox, expecting an instant apology and promises to change. It turns out he couldn't have cared less. "Fine, take it away . . . I don't care!" And I guess he didn't much care because he still hasn't asked for it back.

Here's the Solution

Expressing anger and disappointment and meting out punishment is only the first step in effectively changing your teen's behavior. Helping him figure out what got in the way and finding alternative choices for a more positive outcome is even more important. Case in point: A 14-year-old high school freshman boy, who was a very talented athlete, was invited to join the varsity lacrosse team at his high school. He was the youngest member on the team by several years. It was the night of the first team dinner, and off he went with his older teammates, who chauffeured him to the dinner. Later in the evening, his parents received a call from a neighbor saying that he had been at their local liquor store and they had seen their son walking out to a car with a case of beer!

Shocked and furious, they called their son and told him they were on their way to pick him up. Needless to say, the consequences were flying: He was grounded forever, lost the use of his phone, computer, you name it! Expecting remorse from their son, instead they got attitude! And then they called me. Though I completely understood the need to go for the gold standard in punishment, I encouraged them to get calm and have the following conversation: "Obviously we're so disappointed in the choice you made. You could have been arrested, and your life could have been altered in a serious way. But we also want to understand how this happened so that in the future we can keep you from making such a bad decision. We're guessing that these older guys asked you to go in and buy for them and 'take one for the team.' You're tall and older looking, and they figured you could pass for 21, and apparently you did! I'm also guessing that it would have been really hard to say no to these older guys. It must have felt flattering to be their go-to guy. We really do understand what a difficult situation you were put in, and guess what: this kind of thing will happen more and more now that you're in high school. Let's figure out what you could do or say the next time you're faced with a decision that potentially could put you in harm's way."

It's unrealistic to expect that any consequence alone will change your teen's behavior! Especially when most teens know how to play the "consequence game" using attitude and an artful "I don't care" to avoid giving you the pleasure of feeling like you're in control. Consequences are important, but they're only effective when they're partnered with a learning piece. Teens do a lot of crazy, stupid, scary things, because they are impulsive, emotional, and biologically driven to be risk takers. A metaphorical slap on the hand may sting in the moment, but it won't help much the next time this guy is goaded by his older teammates. Rather than just punishing and criticizing when teens screw up, try understanding and problem solving as well. Your teen might actually learn something!

teaching your teen about money management

curbing the teen money pit

76

Here's the Problem

Every year I poll the college students I teach about what they wished their parents had done differently when they were in middle and high school. Surprisingly, most of my students say, "I wish they had taught me how to manage money." Now, as college students, they find themselves in a constant crisis over money. Because of the financial strain of putting a kid through college, many parents rightly let their kids know that if they want spending money they'll have to earn it themselves. Most parents, totally tapped out with tuition and room and board, expect that their teen's summer job earnings will become first-semester petty cash accounts. For many students, this is the first time they've ever had a finite amount of money to manage for spending. They take out their debit card expecting that magic money will appear, just like their magic phones, their magic gassed-up cars, and their magic college tuition. It can be a rude awakening the first time a card is rejected from the ATM with a resounding NO MORE MONEY! For some kids this may be the first time they can't talk their way into or out of something. No money means no money. It's an ultimate consequence. Unless of course a phone call to Mommy and Daddy succeeds in getting them to deposit a wad of cash in the teen's account with the pro forma "I promise I'll never ask you again." Yeah, right, until the next time.

Why It's a Problem

Many parents I work with often ask me whether they should give their teen an allowance. When kids are young, preschool through elementary school, allowances work really well. It's a great option for parents who are sick of their kids' constant "Can you buy me" whine. Now your go-to response can be "You can buy that toy with the money that you've saved from your allowance." At that age, kids actually love the feeling of saving. So giving your child a small amount of weekly cash teaches the value of money and that saving is important. Kids love to count it, and they constantly update you with their balance. It's a way of defining themselves. *I'm a person who has $53.31 in my savings account.*

Allowance doesn't work this neatly with adolescents. You wonder what happened to your little banker who was once so motivated by that growing bank account full of allowance money, gift money, and money earned from little jobs. But instead of wanting a $5 action figure, now it's a $150 video game, or a $150 pair of jeans, or $150 concert tickets. Money in, money out. Your miserly 10-year-old is all grown up and thinks it's stupid just to let that money sit in the bank when it can be put to good use for something cool.

Allowance has different definitions in different families. Some parents feel that their kids should earn their allowance: If you empty the dishwasher every day that will earn you $2.00 a week; if you clean your room, that earns you another $2.00 a week; take out the trash, another $2.00.

My problem with this is that these are "jobs" that keep a family running. And from my perspective, you don't pay someone to be part of a family.

On the other hand, there may be jobs that you hire out for, like painting a room, cleaning a garage, or landscaping. I think it's appropriate to offer these jobs in-house. If you have teens that need money for the extras, like expensive jeans or video games, this gives them an opportunity to earn the money to buy them.

As kids get older, money takes on a new meaning. They do actually need money on a daily basis for lunch, transportation, entertainment, food, etc. I don't see this as allowance money, but it's still important for them to learn how to manage the money it takes to live a life. Rather than a weekly allowance, I think using a money-management approach is a much more valuable lesson.

Here's the Solution

Most middle school and high school kids are on a pay-as-you-go plan. As in "going to the mall, can I have some money?" Or "going to the movies, can I have some money?" Or "going to hang in town, can I have some money?" Or "I need lunch money, bus money, gas money, school supplies money, clothes money. . . ." In busy families, doling out money can become mindless and perfunctory. "Ma, I need some money!" "What do you need it for?" "A bunch of us are . . . blah, blah, blah." You say OK and open your wallet. Talk about a classic reinforcement schedule. No wonder college students just expect that there will be an endless supply of cash at the push of a button!

Here's a strategy that will prepare your teens *now* to learn how to manage their money in the future, so that you'll avoid getting those panicked college calls. Over the course of the next month, keep a tally of all the money you give to your teen. This should include lunch and transportation money, clothes and incidentals, food, entertainment, and general running-around money. You should definitely make your teen aware of what you're doing and why you're doing it, which by the way is to teach money-management skills. Your teen will not jump for joy and won't want to take responsibility for keeping this tally. This would be an unrealistic expectation. Teens are distracted and forgetful and are probably not all that motivated to change the way things are. They're very happy with the pay-as-you-go model. Remember, it's college students lamenting *after* the fact that they "wished" that they had been better prepared.

Once you've calculated the amount from this monthlong tally, it's time to come up with the plan. Now you must include your teen in the process. Decide how you will mete out this cash, weekly or monthly. Perhaps you'll decide that your teen should manage food, entertainment, transportation, and weekend spending money, but not big-ticket items like clothes. Whatever it is, deposit this agreed-on amount into a debit account. Teach your teen how to check bank balances. Remember, teens use a lot of magical thinking. They may take out $20 here and $20 there and not remember even taking the money out or what they spent it on. THIS IS THE POINT. We get that they're mindless. This is the time now, in a protected environment, to teach mindfulness about money. Maybe every Wednesday night you and your teen go on the bank website and check the balance together. You can help figure out the weekend spending budget. This helps kids to keep track.

If you do this regularly then you won't get the "But I don't have any money left, and everyone is going to the movies!" or the "I need new sneakers!" or the "I need a new outfit for the dance!"

The most important part of this plan is consistency and follow-through. It will probably take only one time when your teen wants to go out with friends and realizes that the allotted money has been spent. Tough luck. Your job is to give a little shoulder shrug and say, "Oh, I'm sorry, that must be hard that you've already spent all your money. You're welcome to have your friends here." No lecture is needed. The empty bank account is all that needs to be said. And by the way, if you cave or if you give advances on a regular basis, you're sending a message that your teen doesn't really have to be responsible about money because when it runs out you will send more. And again, this is the point. In order to change behavior, consequences must be consistent and predictable. This is where the hard work comes in.

The payoff will be enormous. The pride teens will eventually feel for being "in charge" and "in control" of their own finances is priceless.

P.S.: Your teen's future spouse will thank you too!

I just don't fit into this family anymore
helping your teen to feel connected

Here's the Problem

Sometimes I get coaching requests from parents who just don't "get" their teen. It's not only the normal teenage angst these parents are struggling with, but also a deeper sense of not understanding or connecting with the real "who" that is their teen. When you first become a parent, you have fantasies and expectations of what your family will be like. You have visions of family ski trips, trips to museums, or Monday night football dancing in your head. And while your kids are growing up, those fantasies may become your family's realities. But now your previously appreciative, enthusiastic nine-year-old is 16 and expresses deep resentment at having to participate in family activities that he has absolutely no interest in and, to be blunt, hates.

Recently a parent told me about her 15-year-old daughter who likes nothing better than to watch cooking shows and bake. Her favorite TV show is *Cupcake Wars*. This family, however, is athletics personified. They have a vacation house in the mountains. In the winter the family skis, and in the nonwinter months they love to hike. Everyone in this family is thin and fit; this 15-year-old is not. She's not fat, but she's not trim and athletic like everyone else in the family. The parents came to me because they were feeling completely disconnected from their daughter. She wasn't doing anything wrong, but she continually separated herself from the family, perpetuating her sense of nonbelonging. Their other children were physically active and participated in sports. These parents were busy coaching and attending and engaging in their other children's lives. Not so much with this daughter. Not surprisingly, she grew surly, argumentative, and angry most of the time.

Why It's a Problem

Adolescence is all about figuring out "who you are." This girl was doing just that, and she was realizing that who she was was nothing like anyone else in her family. This teen literally had a different body type, a different style of physical energy, and completely different interests. As she became a teen, this became glaringly obvious to everyone. The parents, loving their daughter, were doing everything they could to make her feel included . . . in *their* activities. They cajoled her to come hiking with them, offered her a gym membership to get in shape, a dance class, a yoga class, a personal trainer, anything to get her interested in taking care of her body. It was all to no avail. It only seemed to incite the daughter to resist and reject even more.

The truth of the matter is, your kids are not you! Maybe as they move into adolescence they will continue to enjoy and participate in the same family activities as always. This could just be the luck of the draw. Some teens, now at the "buffet of life," start to see options that are more appealing to them, like this teen did. But in her family, not being like them was seen as a rejection rather than a possibility. It was no wonder she seemed angry and resentful. She felt like she had no place in this family!

Here's the Solution

My suggestion was to accept and embrace the interests and perspective this daughter brought to the family. Instead of resenting her for not wanting to join the family hike, why not take her shopping for baking supplies and leave her to bake goodies for the family for when they returned home, starving and craving a snack? Make her the dessert chef. Find ways of not only supporting her interests, but also her contribution to the family. How wonderful when members of a family are different from one another. Variety is the spice of life!

78 successful rule making

sharing the control

Here's the Problem

It's a Friday or a Saturday night, and your teen is getting ready for a night out. You casually, but warily, ask, "So what's your plan for the night?" You've been down this road before, and can predict the unsatisfying answer. She has been down this road a few times herself, and she casually replies, "Ah, I think maybe, not really sure, but I dunno, maybe going over to X's house and then maybe walking into town to get ice cream, and well I'm not really sure, but yeah going to X's house, and gonna see what's up with everyone." This halting, vague recitation takes five minutes to get out, and still you don't have any idea what your teen will be doing, except it definitely is not what you want her to be doing, which is going to one house, staying there, locked in, with a bowl of popcorn, a movie, an alarm system, and a GPS tracking system in the event of a breakout.

Fears of kids roaming the streets in packs, hanging in the woods or local parks, downing copious amounts of alcohol, smoking pot, and having hot, unprotected, hookup sex dance around in your head. And when you wake up from this horrific daydream, the battle begins. So you say with strident conviction, "You know you're not allowed to roam aimlessly. Until I know specifically what your plan is, you're not leaving this house!" And so it goes . . . again. You put your evening plans on hold, afraid to leave the house without knowing the who, what, and where of your teen's evening plans.

Why It's a Problem

Teens insist on being the CEOs of their own lives. If you're still using the top-down management approach as the rule maker, your teen will willingly and gleefully become the rule breaker. This parenting style worked wonderfully when your kids were in elementary school. They wanted to be controlled, and they liked being controlled. It offered them the safety and security they craved, not to mention that they were obsessed with pleasing you by being the best child in the world. Then adolescence hit. Now when you say, "You're going to do your homework from 7:00 p.m. to 9:00 p.m. and there's no television on weeknights, and you're not allowed to go from place to place when you're out with your friends," you're setting up a power struggle. When you shower teens with a litany of rules, you set up a "yes you will/no I won't" dynamic. The bottom line is that we really can't "make them" anymore. Picking up your six-foot, 180-pound son and putting him in his room, or taking the phone out of his hands, is truly not an option. This kind of controlling parent will probably have kids who lie, sneak, and become creatively obsessed with getting around all the rules.

A friend told me this story about a parent she knew. This parent would boastfully tell other parents how "perfect" her daughter was. She would gloat about the rules and expectations her almost-17-year-old daughter followed to perfection: She was not allowed to have passengers in the car while driving; not allowed to have a boyfriend; not allowed to drink or do drugs; and not allowed to go on sleepovers except at one home that had been vetted. The truth was this girl was merrily flouting every single one of these rules. She had become a supreme liar in the process. It turns out she was the biggest lush of all the girls in her group. Not only did she have a boyfriend, but she was having sex with him regularly by sleeping over at his house when her parents thought she was sleeping at the vetted sleepover home. Rules, shmules!

Here's the Solution

When your kids hit adolescence is the time to make a parenting shift. I know it's not easy. You might think, *If it ain't broke, don't fix it.* But parenting a teen is not the same as parenting an eight-year-old. Your teen has her own ideas about how she wants to live her life. Her new brain is telling her that loud and clear, and she wants to make sure that you hear it too. Your job is to invite your teen into the process. In a logical, reasonable, and, most important, respectful way, develop mutually agreeable rules and consequences. Provide a format, structure, and system that engage the thinking part of your teen's brain. When teens feel part of the process, they're more likely to buy into it. A rule made together has a better chance of being followed than rules made for your teen.

What's interesting is that in most cases, parents and teens are not that far apart in agreements about rules and consequences. It's the process that gets in the way. Sharing in the making of a decision rather than dictating the decision will make a huge difference, both in the outcome (teen doing what she needs to do) and in your relationship (getting along better).

Start with an acknowledgment: "I get it. I know you've had a hard week and want to hang with your friends, so let's figure this out together."

Here's a sequence of questions you can use to facilitate this conversation. Remember that these questions can and should be plugged into any conversation with your teen that requires decision making, including school issues; phone, computer, and social networking issues; negotiating around chores; and family responsibilities. It's a very flexible system.

QUESTION 1: What's your plan?
The story I shared in the first section is an example: You are uncomfortable with the nonplan your teen has just given you. Going from house to house, into town, and around is not acceptable.

QUESTION 2: What do you think I'm going to be afraid of?
It's important for them to tell you what they think. Your kids know you very well. And they'll recite with the accuracy of a Shakespearean actor all the reasons you don't want them to have vague plans for the evening. "You're afraid that if we . . ."

If you lecture about all the ills of traveling in packs, it will put your teen on the defensive and perhaps set her up to lie.

QUESTION 3: Yes, I am worried about those things, and I am also worried that XYZ could happen. What are you going to do to make me feel OK about these things?
The ball is now in your teen's court to come up with a plan to address these worries. Not *your* plan, which she'll probably forget or manipulate, but *her*

plan, for which she will take responsibility. For example, maybe your teen says she'll text you whenever they change locations. You can say that makes you feel OK about the *where* part, but how about *what* they're doing? You're worried that kids are going to be drinking. What is she going to do to make you feel OK about that? Keep going back to that question.

QUESTION 4: What's the consequence going to be if you don't follow through on your plan?
This is a very important step. Before she goes out, have her come up with a consequence for lack of follow-through. It will probably sound something like, "If I screw up, then I won't go out next weekend." Your job here is to restate, "OK so if you don't stay in touch me with me in the way you said, or I suspect you've been drinking or doing drugs, then you won't go out next weekend. Is that right?"

DONE! You're off the hook. She's made her plan and you have agreed on the consequences for lack of follow-through. Make sure you write this down on the fridge or somewhere so you don't get hit with "I never said that." Your only job is to say "Well done" if it goes well, and a shoulder shrug or an "I'm sorry it didn't work out for you" if she has to stay home next weekend. No lecture required!

I cannot emphasize enough the importance of putting your teen in the position of taking personal responsibility for her decisions. Share the control with her. Give her an opportunity to tell you what might work. Believe it or not, teens actually like being responsible. Putting them in the position of *being* responsible rather than *telling* them to be responsible gives them a feeling of competence. This framework gives both you and your teen a roadmap for discussion. Remember it's not useful just to get mad when your teen doesn't follow through on something. What *is* useful? Helping her to come up with a plan to do it better the next time. This is how brain connections are made, with the promise of eventual success in the "I can do it all by myself" department.

79 good cop–bad cop
a parenting dilemma

Here's the Problem

When kids are young, arguments between parents tend toward discussions about how each of you think your kids should eat, or how much TV or computer time they should have, or what time they should go to bed. Arguments that parents of teens have with each other tend to get much more personal: "You never say NO!" or "All you ever do is say NO!" or "Why am I always the bad guy?" or "Don't you remember when you were a teen? Can't you just lighten up?"

Worries about your teen's safety and future and his success in life are present in every decision and negotiation you have with him. Differences in personality and parenting style can become especially apparent when parenting your teen with a partner.

Why It's a Problem

Most of us have vivid memories of our own teenage years and the parents who got us through them. Some memories skew toward the awful: "My parents were so rigid and punitive. I never want to be that way with my teen." Or "I got away with everything. My parents were clueless. It's amazing I'm still alive. I'll be much more on top of stuff with my teenager." Or "My dad never took any sh** from us, and I turned out pretty good, so what was good for me will be good for my kids!" You can see the inherent problem here. If you and your partner were parented from opposite ends of the parenting spectrum and are now parenting from those perspectives, and/or your personality styles are completely different, watch out. Your teen will be in hog heaven! There's nothing better for a teen than having parents who are extreme opposites. Because a teen's brain now allows him to analyze his parents and how they parent (your own private couples counselor), he can now figure out who's the best parent to go to for which things. Want to go to a concert and stay out late? Go to the parent who's excited that you love music and feels concerts are a rite of passage. Definitely do not ask the parent who would never let you go out on a school night, thinks the music you love is for drug addicts, and whose only concert experience is the symphony!

This is problematic, not only because your teen is learning how to manipulate his parenting duo, but also because it's a setup for one parent to have more fun and a better relationship with the teen than the other parent, who ends up in the disappointing position of "bad cop." No fair! When two parents are present in the family, both parents should have equal opportunity and access to the good times and bad times of parenting a teenager.

If a teen learns to manipulate a situation to his advantage on the home front, this can become a roadmap for manipulation in other relationships as well, with friends and future coworkers, bosses, and life partners of their own. Teens learn how to manage the world from the people who are closest to them, and you are those people!

Here's the Solution

The most important rule for equal coparenting is to agree that neither of you will give in to the kind of on-demand requests from your teen that will most likely cause conflict in the parental unit. Teens are extremely talented in the art of negotiation. They want an immediate answer, usually in the affirmative. They are not good at delaying gratification. This puts additional pressure on the front-line parent to go ahead and give an answer. But you must resist. Try saying, "Mom [or Dad] and I will get back to you on that. I know you're looking for an immediate answer, and as soon as I can talk with Mom [or Dad], you'll have your answer." When your teen continues to pressure you for an answer, don't say anything. Give a shrug of your shoulders, a smile, and a "We're on it, and we'll get back to you." And that's that. If it's something that's time-sensitive and the other parent isn't at home, let your fingers do the talking. Thank you technology! Obviously this strategy is only for decisions you know are open to question, not the run-of-the-mill "*Can I go hang at Joey's house?*"

Do not ever disagree as a marital unit in front of your teen! Take it outside, into the bathroom, or in the car. Kids love seeing you two fight over this kind of stuff; it can make one or the other parent seem ineffective and powerless. So please, do your own negotiating privately, especially when you have to take defeat. You and your parenting partner may come from two very different places, but respect for each other always, always, needs to be modeled. Even say to your teen after a decision has been made, "You know I really understand why your mom [or dad] was so worried about this. But we talked about it and here's why we came to this decision." You're communicating the importance of understanding another person's perspective, which may not necessarily mean agreement, but respect for differing opinions. This is just one more of those "life lessons" you want to share with your teen.

finding the bliss
with your teen
treasuring the time

Here's the Problem

I know that some of this book is scary. The "stories" I've shared probably mirror some of your own experiences as a parent of a teen: spending a lot of your time and energy staying on top of your teen's academic life, social life, family life, use (and abuse) of technology, and their burgeoning sexuality, just to name a few. I think we often forget to take the time to "stop and smell the roses." Your teen is in full bloom (to continue with the flower metaphor), and I know you take pleasure in this process of "becoming." But it's hard not to get caught up in trying to keep the weeds out of the garden!

Why It's a Problem

Whenever I do a coaching session with parents, obviously we're spending the time looking at the negative: My teen has an attitude, my teen is lazy, my teen won't do his homework, my teen lies, my teen . . . fill in the blank. At the end of every session I always ask the parents to tell me what they like, admire, and love about their teen. It's important to help balance the difficult with the joy.

One parent, whose son was doing badly in school, putting in no effort, told me how proud she was of his ability to be independent, taking public transportation back and forth daily into the city from the suburbs to pursue his passion and interest in sailing. She had been solely focused on his lack of motivation for school, worried that he would be unmotivated and unsuccessful in life. It was important for her to recognize that when her son found something he loved, his motivation and persistence was amazing.

Another parent, discouraged by her daughter's sneakiness and lack of effort in school, told me of how funny her daughter is and how people are drawn to her. This girl has a significant medical problem that she's had to manage, has some learning challenges, and is doing the best she can under difficult circumstances. Mom needed to respect those challenges and her daughter's efforts in just managing her day-to-day life.

Another parent, after spending an hour venting about all the things her son isn't doing, then told me about his love of music and theater. After moving to a new high school, where he knew no one, he had found his place pursuing these interests and making new friends. This showed a promising resilience to change.

And finally the parents who have very high expectations for their daughter academically, which the daughter meets. They have goals for her to pursue her musical talent, playing in an invitation-only orchestra, which the daughter meets. But these parents also have high expectations that she will do chores, keep her room clean, and be perfectly respectful to her parents at all times. In these matters she is less than perfect. And it's these things on which her parents focus, rather than on the qualities of hard work and discipline this teen exemplifies.

Here's the Solution

Are you getting the message? No kid is perfect, not even yours. Perhaps your teen is engaging in risky behaviors that are scaring the hell out of you, or he won't talk to you, or he isn't even trying to reach for his potential, or he's generally unlikable. It's probably been hard to find the joy in the relationship. Believe me, your teen gets your disappointment. And when this disappointment feels pervasive in your relationship, it will become a self-fulfilling prophecy. "If my parents think I'm a loser, then I might as well start being a loser!" It's important to break the cycle.

Maybe you can leave a card or send a text to your teen saying, "I know things have been hard for us lately. I just want to say I love you and I know we'll figure it out." Maybe say something to her that shows you do notice the small stuff. "You're so lucky to have so many wonderful friends in your life. I've noticed what a wonderful way you have with people." Or "You're one funny guy." Teens needs to know that in spite of the hard stuff between you, you love and appreciate who they are and who you know they'll become. Don't we all need that?

Your teen is becoming a whole new person. It's an exciting and wondrous process and you want to be a part of it! Going to their games and cheering them on, being in the audience for their concerts and plays or art exhibitions, are important ways to support and show your love. But just as important is the time you share *with* your teen. If you have a teen with a passion for music, go to concerts with him, listen to his music with him, get to know him through his music. If you have a teen addicted to video games, get into the game! Play with her, create a character with her, and get to know her through her fantasy. If you have a teen obsessed with reality TV shows, or shows you deem stupid, get on the couch with him, and get to know him through the characters he loves. No judgment or sarcasm allowed!

Finding the bliss with your teen means relinquishing "I wish you were more _____" in favor of "I'd like to get to know you better." You might even learn something new about yourself. What a gift! Take some time now to think and write about what makes your teen special and wonderful. And in those moments when you think you can't take it anymore, pull out this list, take a deep breath, and feel the wondrous person that is your teen.

index

about the author

Joani Geltman, MSW, has more than 30 years of experience working with parents, children, schools, and community groups. She is a clinician, parenting coach, college professor, and public speaker. She has given her parenting seminars Adolescent Psychology—The Parent Version; Sexting and Texting, Alcohol and Drugs: What's A Parent To Do? Bullyproofing Your Teen; and Prom Proofing Your Teen at hundreds of schools, and businesses. Joani's unique brand of "infotainment," using humor, storytelling, and sending parents home with a "goody bag" of helpful techniques, makes these seminars popular events. Joani is a go-to media consultant for television, radio, and print. On and off-camera, she provides the most up-to-date commentary on teen behavior and parenting strategies.